Focus Your Faith!

*Reinforce the Strength &
Steadfastness of your Heart!*

Rudi Louw

Copyright © 2014 by Rudi Louw Publishing

(Revised Edition: *"Don't Quit!! Don't Give Up!!"*)

All rights reserved solely by the author. No part of this book may be reproduced in any form without the permission of the author.

Most Scripture quotations are taken from the *Revised Standard Version*, Holy Bible, Thomas Nelson Publishers. Copyright © 1983 by Thomas Nelson, Inc.

Some Scripture quotations were taken from the *New King James Version*, Holy Bible, Thomas Nelson Publishers. Copyright © 1983 by Thomas Nelson, Inc.

All Scripture quotations not taken from the RSV and the NKJV are a literal translation of the Scriptures *based on the heart and thought being communicated in that particular Scripture.*

The Holy Scriptures are just that; HOLY.

Statements enclosed in brackets were inserted into Scripture quotations to add emphasis or to clarify the meaning of what is being said in those Scriptures. *The integrity of God's Word to man was not compromised in any way. Due care and diligence was cautiously exercised to keep the Word of Truth intact.*

Table of Contents

The Marvel of the Holy Bible 5

Acknowledgments 11

Foreword 13

Prayer 19

1. *Bring in the Reinforcements!* 21
2. *Sustain Your Virtue* 29
3. *Steadfastness* 35
4. *Living Beyond Lack* 55
5. *Single-Mindedness* 59
6. *Being Fully Persuaded* 73
7. *Responding Aggressively* 83
8. *God is Able* 93
9. *We Need Each Other* 99
10. *Walking in True Love* 107
11. *Called to a Higher Standard* 143

About the Author 165

The Marvel of the Holy Bible

1. Uninterrupted Theme and Inspired Thought

It took *1,500 years* to compile the Holy Bible, involving *more than 40 different authors*. Yet the theme and inspired thought of Scripture continues *uninterrupted* from author to author, from beginning till end.

2. Absence of Mythical Stories

Compare philosophies and theories about creation in the Middle East, Europe, Asia, Africa, and Latin America and you'll find mythical scenarios: gods feuding and cutting up other gods to form the heavens and the earth, etc.

In ancient Greek mythology, the Greeks see Atlas carrying the earth on his shoulders. In India, Hindus believe eight elephants carry the earth on their backs.

But in contrast, Job, the oldest book in the Holy Bible, declares that, *"God suspends the earth on nothing."(Job 26:7)*

This was said millennia before Isaac Newton discovered the invisible laws of gravity that delicately balance every planet and sun in its individual circuit.

Contrary to every other ancient attempt to give a creation account, *the Holy Bible pictures the creation of the earth in a very scientific manner.*

For example, in Genesis Chapter One, the continents are lifted from the seas, then vegetation is formed and later animal life, all reproducing *'according to its own kind',* **thus recognizing the fixed genetic laws.** In addition, we have the bringing forth of man and woman, *all done by God in a dignified and proper manner, without mythological adornments.*

The balance or remainder of the Holy Bible follows suite.

The narratives are **true historical documents,** *faithfully reflecting society and culture* **as history and archaeology would discover them thousands of years later. Not only is the Holy Bible historically accurate, it is also reliable when it deals with scientifically proven subjects.** It was never intended to be a textbook on history, science, mathematics, or medicine. *However, when its writers touch on these subjects,* **they often state facts that scientific advancement would not reveal, or even consider, until thousands of years later.**

While many have doubted the accuracy of the Holy Bible, time and continued research have consistently demonstrated that the Word of God is better informed than its critics.

3. Intactness

Of all the ancient works of substantial size, the Holy Bible survives intact, against all odds and expectations.

Compared with other ancient writings, the Holy Bible has more manuscripts as evidence to support it than any ten pieces of classical literature combined!

The plays of William Shakespeare, for instance, were written about four hundred years ago, after the invention of the printing press. Many of his original writings and words have been lost in numerous sections, *yet the Holy Bible's uncanny preservation has weathered thousands of years of wars, contradictions, persecutions, fires and invasions.*

Through the centuries Jewish scribes have preserved the Holy Bible's Old Covenant text, **such as no other manuscripts have ever been preserved. They kept tabs on every letter, syllable, word and paragraph.** *They continued from generation to generation to appoint and train special groups of men within their culture* **whose sole duty it was to** *preserve and transmit these documents <u>with perfect accuracy and fidelity</u>.*

Who ever bothered to count the letters, syllables, or words of Plato, Aristotle, or Seneca for that matter?

When it comes to the New Testament, the actual number of preserved manuscripts is so great that it becomes overwhelming. ***There are more than 5,680 Greek manuscripts, more than 10,000 Latin Vulgate manuscripts and at least 9,300 other versions. Further still, there exists an additional 25,000 manuscript copies of portions of the New Testament.*** **No other document of antiquity even begins to approach such numbers.**

The closest in comparison is Homer's <u>Iliad</u>, with only 643 manuscripts. The first complete work of Homer only dates back to the 13th century.

4. Unmatched Accuracy in Predictive Foretelling

The Holy Bible is unmatched in accuracy in predictive foretelling. No other ancient work succeeds in this, or even begins to attempt this.

Other books such as the Koran, the Book of Mormon, and parts of the Veda claim divine inspiration; ***but none of these books contain predictive foretelling.***

This one undeniable fact we know for certain: *While microscopic scrutiny would show up the imperfections, blemishes, and defects of any work of man, <u>it magnifies the beauties and perfection of God</u>. Just as every flower displays in accurate detail the reflection and perfection of beauty, <u>so does the Word of Truth when it is scrutinized</u>.*

Historian Philip Schaff wrote:

*"Without money and weapons, Jesus the Christ conquered more millions than Alexander, Caesar, Mohammad, and Napoleon. Without science and learning, He (Jesus the Christ) shed more light on things human and divine than all philosophers and scholars combined. Without the eloquence of schools, He (Jesus the Christ) spoke such words of life as was never spoken before or since and produced effects which lie beyond the reach of orator or poet. Without writing a single line, He (Jesus the Christ) set more pens in motion and furnished themes for more sermons, orations, discussions, learned volumes, works of art, and songs of praise **than the whole army of great men of ancient and modern times combined**."* (*The Person of Christ*, p33. 1913)

Today, there are literally billions of Bibles in more than 2,000 languages.

Isn't it about time you find out what it really has to say?

Hey listen, the Holy Bible is all about Jesus, the Messiah, the Christ…

…and everything about Jesus Christ is really about YOU!!

Study Tips:

Read 2 Corinthians 5:14, 16, 18, 19, and 21.

In the light of these Scriptures, it should be obvious that, if you want to study the Holy Bible, *you should study it in the light of Mankind's redemption!*

*Feed daily on **redemption realities*** found in the book of Acts, in Romans Chapters One through Eight, and in Ephesians, Colossians, and Galatians, also in 1 Peter Chapter One, 2 Peter Chapter One, James Chapter One, as well as in 1 and 2 Corinthians.

Acknowledgments

I want to acknowledge and thank one of my mentors in the faith, Francois du Toit, for blessing and impacting me with revelation knowledge.

I borrowed the portion on *"The Marvel of the Holy Bible"* from his website: http://www.MirrorWord.net, as students so often feel they have a right to do with things that come from teachers they respect. Just as Galatians 6:6 says, *"Let him who is taught the Word **share in all good things** with him who teaches."*

To all our dear friends and family, for all the love and support, and to all those who helped me with this project:

THANK YOU!

Also, especially to my wife, Carmen;

For keeping me genuine by being my companion in life and partner in ministry,

I love and appreciate you so very much!

Foreword

Thank you for taking the time to read this book.

Let me start off by saying that *I am totally addicted to my Daddy's love for me.*

I am in love with Jesus Christ, *and that is enough for me!*

The love of God is so much more than a doctrine, a philosophy, or a theory. It is so much more and goes so much deeper than knowledge; it way surpasses knowledge.

We are talking heart language here.

I write *to impact people's hearts,* to make them see the mysteries that have been hidden in Father God's heart concerning Christ Jesus, and actually *concerning THEM,* so as to arrest their conscience with it, *that I may introduce them to their original design and to their true selves,* **and present them to themselves perfect in Christ Jesus** *and set them apart unto Him **in love**,* as a chaste virgin.

We are involved with the biggest romance of the ages.

Therefore this book cannot be read as you would a novel: *casually.* It is not a cleverly devised little myth or fable. **It contains** revelation into some things you may or may not have considered before.

It is the TRUTH of God, ultimate TRUTH, and therefore has direct bearing upon YOUR life. **The Word and the Spirit are my witness** *to the reality of these things!*

Be like the people of Berea whom the apostle Paul ministered to in Acts 17:11. Open yourself up to study the revelation contained in this book **to discover for yourself the reality of these things**.

Be forewarned! Do not become guilty of the sins of the Pharisees, **or you too will miss out on the depth of fulfillment God Himself, who is LOVE, wants to give <u>YOU</u>**.

Jesus said of the Pharisees and Sadducees that they strain out every little gnat BUT swallow whole camels. What He meant by that is that *some people seem to have it all together when it comes to doctrine and they love to argue.*

It makes them feel important, but it is nothing other than EMPTY religious and intellectual pride.

They know the Scriptures in and out, and YET they are still so IGNORANT about **REAL TRUTH** *that is only found in LOVE.*

They are still so ignorant and indifferent **towards the things that REALLY MATTER**.

They are always arguing over the use of *every little jot and tittle* and over the meaning and interpretation of *every word of Scripture.*

The exact thing they accuse everyone else of doing though, the precise thing they judge everyone else for, *they are actually doing themselves.* That is **they often downright misinterpret and twist what is being said,** ***making a big deal of insignificant things while obscuring or weakening God's real truth: the truth of His LOVE***.

They are always majoring on minors ***<u>because they do not understand the heart of God</u>*** *and therefore they constantly miss the whole point of the message*.

Paul himself said it so beautifully,

*"…the letter kills but **the Spirit BRINGS LIFE**;"*

*"…<u>knowledge puffs up</u>, but **LOVE EDIFIES**."*

I say again:

Allow yourself to get caught up in the revelation I am about to share.

Open yourself up to study the insight contained in this book, *not only with a desire to gain knowledge, but also with anticipation* **to hear from Father God yourself, to encounter Him through His Word, and to embrace truth, in order to know and believe the LOVE God has for <u>you</u>**, so that you may get so caught up *in it, **that you too may receive from Him LOVES' impartation of LIFE.***

This revelation contains within it the voice and call of LOVE Himself to every human being on the face of this earth. *If you take heed to it, and yield yourself fully to it, **it is custom designed and guaranteed to forever alter and enrich your life!***

"What then shall we say to all these things?

If God is for us who can be against us!

Who shall separate us from the love of Christ?

**Shall tribulation, or distress,
or persecution,
or hunger, or nakedness,
or peril, or sword?**

**No!!!
In all these things**

*we are more than conquerors
through Him who loves us*

For I am fully persuaded
(totally convinced)
That neither death nor life,
nor angels nor principalities
nor powers of any sort,
nor any present circumstances,
nor things to come,
nor any other created thing,
can separate us from the love of God
which is in Christ Jesus our Lord"
~ Romans 8:31, 35, 37-39

Prayer

Thank you Father that Your almighty power is invested in Your Word; **Your omnipotent power is deliberately invested in the seed of Your Word,** *and therefore we know that we are not just dealing with insignificant little Bible principles; mere man-made philosophies and poetry,* **but we're dealing with the very creative power of almighty God as we get into Your Word.**

Father we know that Your power is able to work within us such glory, such excellence, such beauty that our lives will continue to bless You and please You Father.

I thank you for such open ears to hear by those who read this book *that not one of Your Words would fall to the ground void of power,* **but every Word of Yours, Father, will fall into soil ready to produce in Jesus Name!**

Thank you Father.

Amen.

Chapter 1

Bring in the Reinforcements!

For so many years we have put up *with all kinds of weaknesses in ourselves.* We've accommodated so many of them for so long in the sense of just kind of plotting along and being happy with less than the best. And we thought that it's only some guys that really would make it, you know, like the spiritual giants; *they would really have success in their walk with God,* but most of us would just have to drag our feet and carry on.

But I thank God that the revelation of the New Covenant cancels that kind of conviction. **The revelation of the New Covenant inspires us with the knowledge that <u>there's a strength available in God</u>, which God desires for every man and every woman, even the children, *to walk in.***

Hallelujah!

So in this book we're going to discover from the Word what *spirit-strength* is made up of, and how God can <u>increase our strength</u> in the spirit, *so our steadfastness can give Him pleasure.* **I am talking about *yielding to God* and learning <u>how to grow strong</u> in your**

FAITH, <u>and even more importantly</u> in your LOVE.

God knows that what we need in America today, and really in the whole wide world, *is <u>a REAL revival;</u> not just a bunch of hype and soulish excitement.* **We need a revival of *real change in the heart*, of REAL *FAITH* in God; we literally need a revival of *the <u>FAITH OF GOD</u>*, because what we need is REAL <u>*LOVE*</u>. Not the kind of love that embraces sin, *but <u>the God-kind of LOVE</u> where sin and self-centeredness keeps losing ground until it finds no more room to function in our lives!***

I believe that *an inconsistency in our lives,* whether it is in our faith, or in our love, <u>*only reveals spirit-weakness.*</u>

Neither inconsistency nor weakness pleases God. He cannot draw pleasure from it! I am not saying this in legalistic-terms, as if we are under the Law again, and should strive again to try and please God and win His favor. We don't need to do that anymore, amen, God is already pleased with us; He is already as pleased as He is ever going to get. We owe Him nothing amen. His Favor is a gift; it is ever towards us, amen. So I am not saying this to put you back under condemnation again, *but I am saying to you that God cannot draw pleasure from inconsistency and weakness. He doesn't want us inconsistent and weak! He is able to strengthen us, amen! I am saying to you that*

you are able in Christ Jesus to be strong in your spirit* and live the kind of life *that gives God pleasure. And you need to begin to accept that *in your heart;* you need to *begin to believe that* and say to yourself: ***'I can live the kind of life that gives God pleasure. I can be strong of spirit in Christ Jesus.'***

Amen?! Hallelujah!

So first let us deal with the strengthening of our faith, and then with the strengthening of our love. In 2 Peter 1:3-8, there is an interesting statement made that I want us to look at. You should know this verse off by heart, and meditate in it daily.

2 Peter 1:3-8,

*"His Divine power **has given to us everything needed** for life and godliness;"*

"…through the knowledge of Him;"

"…who called us to His own glory and virtue."

"By these things (by His Divine power; by His glory and virtue) *He thus gave us His precious and very great promises* (His gospel TRUTH; His eternal redemption realities brought about in Christ Jesus);*"*

*"…**so that by them*** (by His own glory and virtue revealed, by His Divine power on display in Christ Jesus, by insight and understanding into the truth of the gospel, by grasping what is

revealed in Christ Jesus, by that revelation into redemption realities) ***you become partakers of the Divine nature*** *and escape the corruption that is in the world because of lust."*

*"Therefore **for this very reason** <u>make every effort to supplement (**reinforce**) your faith with virtue</u>, and virtue with knowledge;"*

"…and knowledge with self-control, and self-control with steadfastness, and steadfastness with godliness;"

"…and godliness with brotherly kindness (mutual affection)*;"*

"…and brotherly kindness with love (God's love; unselfish, sacrificial, abundant love, agape)*."*

"For if these things are yours and are increasing (abounding)**;"**

"…<u>they keep you from</u> being ineffective and unfruitful in the knowledge of our Lord Jesus Christ."

Verse 3,

*"His Divine power has granted to us **all things necessary** for life and godliness **<u>through the knowledge of him</u>** who calls us to his own glory and virtue…"*

Verse 5,

*"…Therefore **for this very reason** <u>make every effort to</u> supplement **(to reinforce)** *your faith…"**

You see, **your faith is your first access to God. Your faith is your first contact with God.** It is when you hear *"the word of truth;" the truth of the gospel, and something is quickened within you* that says to you, *'This is worth its credit;* **this truth that I've heard is worth my yielding to it!'** *That is when your faith now links you to everything that God has granted to you* **that is needed for life and godliness.**

God made available to you **every possible energy that you would ever need to draw from** to be a strong person in Christ Jesus. **But now it's your faith that links you and plugs you into that energy resource of strength and enablement and empowerment.**

Notice there in Verse 5 he says,

"Therefore <u>for this very reason</u> **make every effort to supplement (to reinforce)** *your faith…"*

Your *faith* speaks of your personal relationship with *"the **Word of truth**," with "the **Word of God**," with "**the truth of the gospel;**" "**the truth of redemption**".*

In Verse 1 he says,

"To those who have obtained (as a gift) ***a faith of equal standing with ours*** *in the righteousness of our God and savior Jesus Christ."*

You see, this faith has **an equal standing before God.** It means that it also, therefore, *has **an equal potential.*** It means that **you can enjoy God** *as much as I can enjoy Him.* It means that ***you have the ability*** **to obey Him** *as much as I have the ability to obey Him.* It means that **you can have as much of God in your life as I can have in my life.** It means that you and I **can have as much of God in our lives** *as any of the apostles even could have in their lives.* <u>Every person on this planet</u> **can walk in the same quality of intimacy with God, as the apostles enjoyed; as Paul enjoyed, even as Jesus Himself enjoyed, because there's an** *equality* **in faith that** *gives us equal access* **to every blessing of God**

Another translation of that same 2 Peter 1:1 says that, *"...**you have obtained like precious faith together with us, the apostles**, through the righteousness of God and our savior Jesus Christ,"* and Paul goes on to even say in 1 Corinthians 1:9 that, *"We have been called in the fellowship of the Son;* (the exact same fellowship the Son Himself enjoyed and still enjoys).*"*

But now we often see that ***not everybody is enjoying equal bliss and blessing in God.***

Why are so many people living so far below *the standard of blessing, the standard of bliss that God desires for them?* The author of Hebrews writes and he says in Chapter 6 that,

"I am convinced that there is much more that belongs to your salvation."

I share the same conviction. **I am persuaded that there is so much more for us to enjoy than most have entered into, or ever even realized that they could!**

So here in 2 Peter 1:5 Peter encourages us with these words,

"Therefore **for this very reason** *make every effort to supplement* (**to reinforce**) *your faith* **with virtue.***"*

I want you to know he is not talking about *"making every effort"* **in your own strength and energy, in your own will power.**

'So Rudi, if he is not talking about **my own efforts** *then what is he talking about?'*

Chapter 2

Sustain Your Virtue

We need to ask a question: What is that "***virtue***" he is referring to?

He is talking about **God's Divine power:** *His energy, His strength, and His enablement which He enables us with.* **He is talking about** *the expression* **of our faith,** *the expression of God's character and nature in our very lives.*

Listen; <u>virtue</u> takes faith out of theory *and puts it <u>into the practical</u>.* **It brings faith right** *into the reality of our day-to-day living.*

Then he goes on to say,

"...supplement (**reinforce**) *your faith with virtue and virtue with knowledge."*

Because *your faith and that virtue available to you through it, must now be* **sustained** through **the knowledge of Him;** *through the Word of God, through the gospel, through the truth you've heard in the Word of TRUTH; that truth concerning the work of redemption.*

You see, it is one thing to have **a sudden expression of God in your life,** or to have **a great breakthrough** in your life ***for a moment.***

God wants to sustain that expression; He wants to sustain that expression of His character and nature in your life; **He wants *to sustain* that virtue (that energy, that enablement, that strength, that power) that is yours in Christ Jesus!**

The blessing of God; that bliss we enjoy, as well as the *"**virtue**"* of God (that strength, energy, and power; that enablement *to express your faith continually*) **is not by accident.**

*It's not **by accident*** that you, as a believer, from time to time, feel the presence of God and that you feel His anointing.

So often we wrongly think that *the presence and anointing of God;* that the blessing of God - that bliss with God, and that strong faith – *the kind of faith that changes things,* is only something to be experienced *from time to time.*

I mean, brother Rudi, *'**We never really know when**, you know, but just **from time to time; it is almost as if it's by accident** that we as believers have a special anointing or a special breakthrough **from time to time**.'*

What a bunch of nonsense. With that kind of reasoning it is no wonder that your expression of faith is inconsistent at best, and that you live most of your life in defeat!

Listen; I believe that **God wants His virtue, His energy, His strength, His enablement, His power; the very expression of His character and nature in you - He wants that faith of equal standing to that of the apostles,** *to be something we experience and express and live in* <u>*all the time*</u>.

You see, Verses 3 and 4 speak of us being,

"...partakers of His Divine nature."

But what's the use of being a partaker of God's nature *if I cannot express that nature* ***consistently?***

I believe that that *expression* of that nature <u>has everything to do</u> with that little word *"**virtue**"* (energy, enablement, strength, power) **that completes my faith.**

And so, because of that he says in 2 Peter 1:5,

"Supplement (**reinforce**) *that virtue* **with** *knowledge..."*

Not just any kind of knowledge, but the kind of knowledge *that would feed your spirit with the ability* <u>to continue to express God</u> **in your life.**

He is talking about **the knowledge of** *the New Testament;* **the knowledge of** *the New Covenant.* He is talking about **revelation knowledge into the truth of the gospel; that exact knowledge of** *THE TRUTH as it was* *revealed in Jesus Christ and His work of Redemption.* He is talking about **the knowledge of** *the New Creation;* **the knowledge of** *Righteousness by Faith.* He is talking about **the knowledge of** *our Salvation;* **the knowledge** that *he who is joined to the Lord is ONE SPIRIT with Him.* He is talking about **the knowledge of** *our acceptance in the Beloved;* **the knowledge of** *our Father's extravagant love for us,* **of** *our Identity,* **of** *Sonship.* He is talking about **the knowledge that** *I am a partaker of the Divine Nature.* He is talking about **the knowledge of** *our victory over the enemy; of freedom from the dominion of sin.* He is talking about **the knowledge of** *our absolute authority.*

You see, the very Love Nature of God himself has been *awakened* **in my heart, in my inner-man,** *by the Holy Spirit of Truth, through the truth of the gospel.* *He has had access to my spirit all along, in fact it is Him personally who has opened my spiritual eyes to see these things,* **and now since I have yielded to Him and embraced His working in my inner-man, He has made His home in me.** It is no longer I, merely living my life, trapped in my natural identity, *but it literally is Christ who lives in me now;* <u>*I have been awakened to my true spirit-identity*</u>*! I have been awakened to likeness and to oneness!* **I have been awakened to the fact that** *I am one Spirit with Him! There is no separation between Him and me, ever!* Any thought of

somehow being separate *is a lie!* ***Separation is a lie! Union and Oneness is my portion! In Him I live and move and have my being! My life is hid with Christ in God!***

That's the only kind of **knowledge** *that would feed your spirit* **with <u>the ability to continue to express God</u> *in your life.***

Hosea 4:6,

*"My people are destroyed for **lack of knowledge**;"*

*"…because **they have rejected knowledge.**"*

Chapter 3

Steadfastness

He goes on to say in Verse 6,

*"Supplement (**reinforce**) that knowledge **with self-control.**"*

That means I am not going to allow the enemy <u>**to interrupt my expression**</u> **of Jesus, my expression of His image and likeness, my expression of His Divine Nature that resides in my spirit!** It means **I'm going to control myself** even when the enemy wants to use my natural-minded-self to go in opposition or in rebellion **to the truth of God that resides within me.** I will control my **Self.** I will control **the flesh.**

What is **FLESH** or **SELF** made up of?

It is made up of **your natural identity, or *your identity in the flesh.***

The **FLESH** and **SELF** is made up of **natural minded passions and desires.** It is made up of the **lust** of the eyes, the **lust** of the flesh, and the **pride** of life.

The word **lust** means **strong desires.**

Proverbs says that a person that is without **Self-control** is like a city **that is broken into and left without walls**. That means that protection which protects and shields and shelters my spirit is broken down.

But **Self-control,** we read in Galatians 5, is *a fruit* of the spirit. **And *fruits* are produced through consistent fellowship, *consistent, intimate fellowship* with God and His Truth!**

1 Peter 2:11,

"Flee youthful (immature, childish) *lusts* (strong desires) **which war against the soul."**

So, these youthful (immature, childish) lusts, **this FLESH thing, this natural minded SELF thing *<u>is an outside force</u>* which wars against your soul.**

But how does it **gain entrance** *into your heart?* Why do I end up *being controlled by it?*

It only gains entrance, and you end up being controlled by it, only because of an **ignorant spirit,** a **blind spirit;** a **weak**, or **sick**, or **immature spirit -** a spirit that is **lacking,** a spirit that **has not been <u>reinforced</u> with the knowledge of the TRUTH -** a spirit that has been **polluted by other influences which contradict the truth of the Word, the truth of the gospel;** *redemption realities.* I am talking about influences that **do not come from God! I am talking about a spirit trapped in darkness, a spirit *full of***

ignorance, confusion and deception. (See 2 Corinthians 4:3–4; Galatians 3:23; 4:1–5; Colossians 3:5–7, 9–11; Ephesians 4:17–24; 5:8; 1 Peter 2:7–9)

2 Corinthians 6:17, 18 & 7:1 clearly declares,

"Therefore 'Come out from among them and be separate, says the Lord. ***Do not touch what is unclean,*** *and I will receive you.'"*

"I will be a Father to you, and you shall be My sons and daughters, says the Lord Almighty."

7:1 *"Therefore, having these promises…"*

(A better interpretation would be, ***"having this reality to enjoy."***)

"…beloved, ***let us cleanse ourselves <u>from all filthiness</u> of the flesh <u>AND SPIRIT</u>, perfecting holiness*** *in the fear of God (in reverence and respect and appreciation and adoration of the radiant countenance of God revealed in Christ)."*

Being cleansed from all filthiness of the flesh and of the spirit ***through the truth;*** through revelation knowledge - *through insight and understanding into the truth of the gospel,* ***into redemption realities*** *is what holiness is all about!*

Let's continue to read in 2 Peter and see what else Peter has to say about this subject of *cleansing the spirit* and *perfecting holiness* **in appreciation and adoration of the radiance of God's person displayed so clearly in Christ.**

2 Peter 1:6,

"...Supplement (**reinforce**) *self-control* **with STEADFASTNESS..."**

This little word *"steadfastness"* is the word I want us to concentrate on in our study of God's Word in this book.

"STEADFASTNESS..."

Steadfastness is the definition of *the quality of your spirit.* **It reveals <u>the strength</u> of your spirit.**

<u>Inconsistency</u> or <u>unstableness</u> would reveal a *weakness* of spirit.

But God wants us to be <u>strong in spirit</u> so that the steadfastness of <u>His strength within us</u> will continue *to sustain the virtue* (the energy, the enablement, the power and strength)*, the very life of Jesus, that expression of Jesus in and through us, that holiness – that like precious faith, that pure faith of equal standing with that of the apostles.*

Let's turn to James 1:2,

James says,

*"Count it all joy my brethren **when you meet various trials**..."*

Now this is bad news to some *because they think that the walk of the believer is going to somehow lock them into a nice little bubble and they'll never face any trials or tribulation; they'll just continue on in bliss and be hidden away in this little bubble until Jesus comes.* But the truth is: *"...many are the afflictions of the righteous,"* because you see, **the enemy targets them.**

But thank God that's not all that was written there. He goes on to say,

*"...**but out of <u>them all</u>**..."*

Not 90% of them. No!

"...out of them <u>all</u>..."

That means 100% of them!

"...out of them <u>ALL</u>..."

*"...<u>**God**</u> delivers them."*

Hallelujah!

So every affliction that comes your way is **an opportunity for you (by you sustaining and reinforcing your faith) to experience again the deliverance of God!**

Amen!

Let's continue on in James 1:2,

"Count it all joy my brethren when you meet various trials;"

*"...<u>for you know</u> that **the testing of your faith produces STEADFASTNESS.**"*

Now before we go on you need to understand that *"the testing of your faith"* **is not from God. *It is not God's work.* It is not God *at work.* It has nothing to do with God. God is not** *"testing your faith."* **He already knows the ingredients of the faith that has once and for all been delivered to the saints! He already knows the ingredients of that faith! God already knows the ingredients of faith; *He doesn't need to test it!* He knows how powerful it is!**

*"...this is the victory that overcomes the world, **even our <u>faith</u>!**"*

NO, IT IS NOT GOD; *IT'S THE ENEMY THAT IS COMING AGAINST YOU.* And he comes against you *to test your steel, to try you*, because he wants what you've got. **He wants the vehicle of your spirit to be his; to be *his trophy.* He wants to possess you for himself, *to own you; to link up with you, so he could use your body and your mind as his vehicle, and exercise his filthy character through you and express himself through you.***

But God has possessed you for Himself, *through His Word, through the truth of His gospel,* and through *the Spirit of Truth!* God has laid ***a stronger claim*** upon your life ***through the resurrection of Jesus Christ; through new creation realities,*** and **He has awakened within you His own nature, *through those new creation realities.***

And so, James the apostle, inspired by the Holy Spirit, says that,

*"…**when you meet** various trials…"*

That means *you will just be walking along life's path **and run into** various different trials.*

It means that *various trials of different nature* would **cross paths with you,** and come against you, *to seek to challenge you;* **to challenge** *that faith - that life that you now have* **in Christ Jesus.**

Those various trials of different nature **seek to challenge** *your faith,* <u>**and they try to neutralize and annihilate your faith**</u>. ***They try to render it powerless, weak, and ineffective,* and for all practical intents and purposes render it <u>*useless*</u> when it comes to life in the here and now.**

But James says in James 1:3,

*"…the testing of your faith **produces STEADFASTNESS.**"*

Do you see that steadfastness is **produced?**

Steadfastness is **produced** *out of your inner being,* **out of your fellowship with God's truth; with the truth of the gospel.**

Steadfastness is **produced out of your fellowship around God's love for you demonstrated in Christ; out of your intimate fellowship with God Himself.**

Like a tree produces fruit, steadfastness is **produced out of your spirit,** and we have seen earlier that we are to, *"supplement* (or to **reinforce**) *our knowledge **with self-control**."*

That means we are standing as individuals responsible, *at least to some degree,* **for our stability.**

Now I know we don't like to hear that. We would like the pastor to be responsible, and Jesus to be responsible, and anybody else **but us** *to be responsible for our stability.* And God has taken that responsibility upon Himself to strengthen us with might by His Spirit, by the Spirit of Truth in our inner-man; *through revelation knowledge into the truth of the Gospel.* God has covenanted with Himself to do that; God is faithful, amen! God watches over His word to uphold it and perform it! Nobody can deny that. God uses His word; He uses the truth of the gospel to enlighten us and strengthen us and uphold His work in our lives; in our inner-most being. *"He who has begun a good work in us is faithful to complete it to the* *uttermost in the day of the Lord Jesus Christ; in the light of the successful work of redemption; until it is fully established in us! He is able to perform that work and uphold it for all of time and eternity!"* - Philippians 1:6. Amen! Hallelujah! But we have our part to play in it; **WE HAVE BEEN GIVEN AUTHORITY, BY GOD, THROUGH THE TRUTH OF THE GOSPEL,** *AND SO **WE** ARE, TO SOME DEGREE, RESPONSIBLE FOR **OUR OWN** STABILITY.*

Nobody else is responsible for **your steadfastness**. You can hold nobody else responsible **for your spiritual strength**. **YOU** are ultimately standing, to some degree, responsible for these things! **The Word produces it**, <u>***but it is your embrace of the Word***</u> *that is the key to the whole thing!*

Paul says to Timothy,

*"**Train yourself** in godliness."*

You see, you could have the best tutoring, *the best instruction, and you can hear the best Word; **the truth of the gospel most accurately.*** But until you come to a place where you <u>take that word that you've learned *and put it into practice in your life*</u>, you'll never develop in *spirit strength* and energy and STEADFASTNESS.

It is amazing to me how people can sit under the greatest word <u>*and still live in sin*</u> and still live *weak spiritual lives!*

STEADFASTNESS has everything to do *with the condition of your spirit,* *with your spirit's **fitness** in Christ Jesus.*

You see, I can go and read all the books on physical fitness that I like, ***but until I fully embrace and begin to <u>activate</u> that knowledge*** and begin to go and work out in the gym, or go run on the road somewhere, I will never know what real physical fitness is.

I say again: **Your spirit's fitness in Christ Jesus *is directly related to your STEADFASTNESS.***

STEADFASTNESS reveals *the condition of your spirit.* What is the condition of <u>your</u> spirit? Do you have a *weak, sick, and anemic* spirit?

STEADFASTNESS is <u>*produced*</u> *from within you <u>by the abiding TRUTH of the gospel</u>*!

James says here in James 1:2–3 that,

"...when you meet various trials,"

(...when you are *tested by the enemy*;

...when you are *tried* by the enemy,

...and *face various contradictions to your faith,*)

*"...<u>**it's an opportunity** for that steadfastness to become manifest;</u>"*

"...to be produced from within you."

STEADFASTNESS is **produced from within you by the abiding WORD.** It's produced *by the abiding TRUTH of the gospel!*

King Solomon, under inspiration of the Holy Spirit instructed, (not just his son, but all of us as well) **to abide in the Word**.

"...for it is life to those who find it;"

He says that,

"...from it spring the issues of life."

Let's read it. Proverbs 4:20–23,

*"My son, **give attention** to my Word;"*

*"**Incline your ear** to my sayings."*

*"**Do not let them depart** from your eyes;"*

*"**Keep them** in the midst of your heart;"*

(**Treasure it** in other words)

*"For it is **life** to those who find it,"*

"...and (even) health to all their flesh."

*"**Keep** (guard the focus of) **your heart** with all diligence;"*

(In other words: Protect the environment of your heart. Don't just embrace any old word, or teaching, or doctrine. Embrace the truth of the gospel, see it for the treasure it is, and don't allow any contradictory thought to that truth of the gospel to come into your mind. Don't allow any other thought-pattern or mindset to rule and reign your heart, other than a thought-process inspired by the gospel)

*"…for out of it **spring** the issues of life."*

Jesus also said something similar in John 15:4–5,

*"**Abide** in Me, and I in you."*

*"As the branch <u>cannot bear fruit of itself</u>, **unless it abides** in the vine;"*

*"…neither can you unless you **abide in Me**."*

"I am the vine, you are the branches."

*"He who **abides in Me**, and I in him, **bears much fruit**;"*

"…<u>for without Me you can do nothing</u>."

He says in Verse 2 and Verse 6,

"Every branch in Me;"

"…<u>that does not bear fruit;</u>"

"He takes away (A better translation would be: **He lifts it up** off the ground and **sure it up** or **strengthens it**. He removes the very thing,

the very thought-process; the very mindset that negatively influences that branch and causes it not to bear fruit);"

"…and every branch that bears fruit;"

"He prunes;"

"…that it may bear more fruit."

(That pruning; that **strengthening of the branch,** which causes it to bear more fruit, comes through the truth of the gospel and nothing else. That truth of the gospel; deep speaks unto deep, and it impacts the heart, and separates from and removes from the branch every draining, energy stealing influence, because it does not belong, and it competes with the growth and fruit-bearing of that branch; of that person.)

"If <u>anyone</u> does not abide in Me;"

"…he is disconnected as a branch <u>and is withered</u>;"

He says in Verse 3,

*"You are **<u>already clean</u>** (pruned) **because of the word** which I have spoken to you."*

That means: If you ignore that word; **if you ignore the truth of the gospel** there is a good chance *you will need cleaning up again!* ***Do not allow yourself* <u>to become polluted again in your spirit</u> *by some other influence.***

In John 17:17 He prayed,

*"**Sanctify them** (clean them, set them apart, make them strong in spirit) **by Your truth.**"*

*"**Your word is truth.**"*

How do we **abide** in Jesus?

1 John 2:5, 24–27,

*"But whoever **keeps** (embraces, believes, treasures, and holds on to) His Word;"*

*"…<u>**truly the love of God has come to completion in him**</u>."*

*"**By this** <u>we know</u> that we are in Him."*

By this we awaken to oneness, to our union with Him; to His indwelling. **By this** we **abide** in Him; we become conscious of His abiding presence within us!

(BY THIS <u>we know</u> - **When we believe and embrace His Word, the truth of the gospel, <u>WE KNOW</u>, we intimately know, we awaken to the reality THAT <u>WE ARE IN HIM</u>!**)

*"Therefore let **that** (**let that word**) **abide** in you (that truth; that gospel);"*

*"…**which you heard from the beginning.**"*

*"If what you heard from the beginning (If the truth of the gospel, **the truth of God's love for**

us; the truth of what was in God's heart concerning us from the very beginning, from before time even began, *if that truth, that WORD*) **abides in you;"**

"...<u>you also will abide</u> in the Son and in the Father."

Jesus was all about the WORD of God. He was that WORD **made flesh.** That WORD, that *"LOGOS"* of God; His thoughts, His opinion, His truth, His eternal intimate knowledge of who He is to us, and who we are to Him; *who He really is and who we really are,* **became incarnate.**

That means: **God and Man became manifested in one body!**

He, God the Son, took on flesh and blood and revealed both the true identity and nature of the Father, *and therefore the true design; the true identity and nature of Man,* **in one body.**

Jesus was and is that authentic, original image and likeness **we are made in; the very image and likeness of God,** *on display!*

From the beginning to the end He proclaimed to us *the word of the Father;* the word that was *in the heart of the Father,* the LOGOS that was from the beginning; that Word, that LOGOS that was in the Father; that LOVE MESSAGE, the TRUTH, the GOSPEL that was in the heart of the Father from the very beginning.

"But the anointing **(the virtue, the energy, the enablement, the strength, the power)** *which you have received from Him* **abides** *in you* **(through the word, through the knowledge of Him, through the truth of the gospel)** *... and you do not need that anyone teach you;* **But** *(or because)* **as** *the same anointing* (the same Word, the truth of the gospel; that truth that was from the beginning, which you received from Him, **as** *that same anointing,* **as** *that same interaction with the Spirit of Truth*) **teaches you** *concerning all things,* **and is truth***, and is not a lie, and so now,* <u>**just as it has taught you**</u>*, you will* **abide** *in Him."*

What does our interaction with the Spirit of Truth teach us? That we **HAVE the VICTORY!** That we **must** *abide* in Him. He teaches us; that anointing teaches us, that interaction with the Spirit of Truth teaches us that we **cannot afford** *to ignore* **the truth of God's Word made flesh;** *that truth of the gospel!*

Why?

Because our VICTORY – our *freedom from* **sin's dominion, the** *strength* **of our faith, the** *strength* **of our spirit; our very lives** *depend on it!*

Paul said in 1 Thessalonians 2:13,

"<u>For this reason</u> we also thank God without ceasing;"

*"...because **when you HEARD** the Word of God;"*

*"...**you RECEIVED it;**"*

*"...and **WELCOMED it;**"*

"...not as the word of men;"

*"...but **as it is in truth;**"*

"...the very Word of God;"

*"...which **now** also **effectively works** in you who BELIEVE."*

James further encourages us in James 1 when he said in Verse 4,

*"And **let** steadfastness have **its full effect**."*

STEADFASTNESS of spirit will affect your life positively **more than anything else.**

In James 5 the apostle James makes reference to Isaiah 55, and he speaks about the farmer who waits patiently for the rain to come, *because he knows that the seed is in the ground, and that that seed will be awakened to newness of life, to life more abundantly, to the fullness of life; it will be awakened to the fullest, by that rain.* The farmer **doesn't tolerate and allow anything to cover the ground and block the rain, neither does he tolerate or allow anything to disturb the seed. And he does not dig**

the seed up every now and then to try and measuring the little seed, or measure the growth of the seed. He is just letting his own steadfastness, his own patience, have its full effect, *so that the full fruit can manifest!*

Don't let the enemy interrupt what God is working in your spirit and in your life. Embrace the rain, embrace the word; embrace the gospel fully. *Let* steadfastness have *its full effect*.

Why?

James 1:4,

*"...**that you may be perfect and complete, lacking in nothing**."*

God's ultimate for your life is to be, *"...perfect and complete, lacking in nothing."*

*To be **"perfect and complete, lacking in nothing,"* need not be an experience that only some of us *might have* one day in* Heaven.

Listen; *I fully believe that **this is the standard and the quality of life God wants us to live and enjoy now**.*

I am talking about **the quality** of your faith walk and your love walk. I am talking about *experiencing* your faith **consistently**, *experiencing* the love of God **consistently** in your life, **24/7**, and then also *expressing* your faith **consistently,** *expressing* the love of God **consistently** through your life, in **all** **circumstances** and in **all** **situations.**

I am talking about **steadfastly** living your life ***in the sustained experience of God's nearness,*** *which only redemption realities affords you!*

Steadfastly live your life by those unshakable redemption realities!

I am talking about ***living 1 Corinthians 13 out loud!*** I am talking about ***consistently experiencing*** and ***steadfastly living out*** *THE TRUTH of the gospel!*

Actually live out *Jesus' Sermon on the Mount* in Matthew 5, 6 & 7, **whether you feel like it or not!** I am talking about *being a **real** Christian, **full of faith and love, no matter what!***

I am talking about being so in love with your Daddy God that *you actually say no to sin.*

I am not saying that *you will get it right every single time,* and that you will *never make a mistake,* but that **you will get better at** *expressing* **who you are in Christ Jesus and expressing who you really are in Him** *more* **consistently!**

Let God become the source of your strength. *Let God's love become your* *inspiration, your empowerment and your strength.* **YOU <u>CAN</u> say no to sin! You don't have to live in defeat and weakness, you CAN overcome.**

IF you do make a mistake, **IF** you do miss it, not **WHEN** but **IF** you do mess up, you immediately get yourself up out of the mud. You scrape yourself up off the floor and dust yourself off and stand up like a man and make a course correction.

I am talking about determining in your spirit that you are going to live a victorious life, <u>consistently and STEADFASTLY</u>!

Chapter 4

Living Beyond Lack

James 1:4,

*"And **let** steadfastness have **its full effect;**"*

*"…**that you may be perfect and complete, lacking in nothing**."*

This scripture says **it can be ours, *but it comes through STEADFASTNESS* having its full effect in my life.** I will always be conscious of lack, conscious of my own imperfection, of my own failure, of my own disappointments **while I live in inconsistency;** *in double-mindedness,* **lacking in steadfastness of faith.** But when steadfastness **has its full effect, *it produces within me* a strength of spirit that causes me to live beyond *sin*, beyond *lack*, and beyond *disappointment!***

Now I believe that that's *the standard of life, the very quality of life* that God desires **for each one of us to enjoy and live in.**

I want us to notice something in Psalm 125:1–2. It says, *"Those who **trust** in the Lord are like mount Zion **which cannot be moved.**"*

*"As the mountains are round about Jerusalem **so the Lord is round about His people** from this time forth and forevermore."*

What makes us, *who trust in God,* like mountains? The fact that a mountain cannot be moved but *abides* forever!

Psalm 125:2,

*"**As the mountains are** round about Jerusalem **so the Lord is round about His people from this time forth and forevermore.**"*

You see, **God wants to be that strength within you** which causes you to stand firm and steadfast like a mountain. Not just standing firm against sin, *but in any kind of situation!*

That kind of strength and steadfastness belongs to those *who **trust in** (rely on, draw from) the Lord*.

"Trust in the Lord" **speaks of your relationship with His Word,** *with the truth of His Word.* Your *"Trust in the Lord"* reveals **whether you understand and believe the integrity and reliability of His Word** *or not.*

How can you *measure* your trust in God?

You can only measure it by your relationship with His Word; *with the truth of the gospel.* Because God has given His Word to you, He has fully revealed His heart

to you in Christ, and that gospel reveals **the integrity of His purpose.** And He says His faithfulness *is steadfast.* **God's faithfulness speaks of _His_ relationship to His Word;** *to the truth of the gospel.*

You see, here in this Scripture and in many others *God's Word expresses His own relationship to His Word.* His **almightiness,** His **strength and enablement,** His **very power and virtue,** his **very anointing _is inseparably linked to His Word; to the truth of the gospel._** And we know that, *"…it's the anointing* **that destroys the yoke."**

God is not standing in a casual way towards His Word. He watches over His Word according to Jeremiah 1:12. **God is intimately engaged in His Word. That makes Him a faithful God. He watches over His word to perform it, to *DO it,* to uphold it *and make it good!***

He says in Psalm 125 that,

*"**They** who trust in the Lord…"*

It speaks of them that now put their relationship, their trust, their confidence **in the unshakable foundation of God's Word;** *the truth of the gospel.*

*"…**they** are like mount Zion."*

How do we get there?

I believe Luke Chapter Six reveals something very important to us. It speaks about **the wise man, who in his wisdom, _dug deep._**

Chapter 5

Single-Mindedness

In Luke 6:47 Jesus said,

*"Everyone that **comes to me** and **hears my words** and **does them;**"*

"…I will show you what he is like."

I want you to see the importance of **a relationship with God's Word; *with what God has declared in Christ, in that incarnation and work of redemption!***

A relationship with God's Word includes two things:

1. It includes **a diligence as far as your hearing is concerned.**

2. And it includes **a diligence as far as your doing is concerned.**

So Jesus says here in Luke 6:47,

*"Everyone who **comes to me** and **hears my words** and **does them** I will show you what he is like…"*

We are getting a look at **those who trust in the Lord** and are like mount Zion, and *who therefore cannot be moved and cannot be shaken.*

"…I will show you what he is like…"

*"…he is like a man building a house, **who dug deep and laid the foundation upon a rock;***

*…<u>when a flood arose and a stream broke lose against that house</u> the stream **could not shake** the house;*

*…**for it was founded on the rock**."*

Can you see that this house could fulfill James 1:2? This house could **count it all joy** when it met with testing from various streams and floods and trials, *because it was founded upon the rock.*

Now in that same Chapter, there is a revelation I want to bring in here. In verse 8 James speaks there of, *"…a **double-minded** man."* He says that this man is, *"…**unstable** in all his ways."*

Would you agree with me that **unstable** is the opposite of the STEADFASTNESS we are discussing in this book?

We are discussing **being strong** in spirit, and being **able to endure in life,** *being able to be perfect and complete, lacking in nothing.*

I want you to appreciate what it means to *build your house upon the rock.*

James speaks of *"a **double-minded** man **unstable** in all his ways."* But I want us to appreciate what it means to **build a house upon the rock.**

I mean, since we were knee high to a grasshopper, we have been singing that little song in Sunday-school: *'You've got to build your house upon a rock. A sure foundation; the Word of God. And the rains may come and go, but the Word of God you will know...'* And we appreciate this Scripture as a beautiful parable that Jesus told. **But how do you build your house upon the rock?** What does Jesus mean by *building your house upon the rock?*

I believe that **building your house upon this rock** means *a single-mindedness, a narrow-mindedness.*

Jesus said in another place,

"Narrow, (or exclusive, or single-minded) *is the way **which leads to life**."*

He also says in that Scripture in so many words that, *"…broad* (or double-minded) *is the way that leads to destruction."*

You see, single-mindedness, narrow-mindedness, is the ingredient *that will release steadfastness* into your heart.

That means you no longer will be moved by any wind of contradiction or anything that comes against you that seeks to blow you over.

That single-mindedness *is produced* through your relationship with - *through your exclusive focus upon the mind of God revealed in His Word of truth; in the truth of the gospel.*

And if that is indeed the case; *if you become single-minded in these things,* then this will be your prayer,

'God I **believe** your Word, I **hear** your Word, **I take heed** to what I hear, and Father as I **hear** your Word **I'm committed to be a consistent doer** of your Word.'

Listen, God is not expecting me to *do* something that I would not have the ability to do. God is only expecting me to **work out** the *salvation which* **He works within, through revelation.** You see because **my doing is in the first place a seeing** through revelation; **a grasping of truth, an unveiling of eternal reality.**

So, **my doing is the fruit of seeing; it's the fruit of insight and understanding into the knowledge of Him!** As I hear His Word I receive the very material that the Holy Spirit would use in this workshop of God; *in my spirit,* **to produce within me that quality of God's**

nature that is expressed as His virtue in my life, amen!

You see; as I build upon that rock, *I begin to single-mindedly give myself to the strength of that rock.* And that rock, that mountain, is not threatened by any wind or any storm or any flood that breaks loose against it. **It cannot be shaken, it cannot be moved.** *It stands unshakably strong.*

Hallelujah!

In that same Chapter of Luke Jesus speaks of another man that also builds a house. And on the outside you couldn't tell the difference. But **the storm <u>reveals</u> the difference**. You see, on the outside we all sit in church and we all look good, we all look nice and we look so pretty. *But the storm <u>reveals</u> the difference.* The storm is many times the only thing that will show you *whether you are a person* **merely deceiving yourself**.

Many precious, sincere Christians today are living lives of deception. And they are *not being deceived by the devil or anyone else for that matter, other than themselves,* <u>**because they fail to link the foundation of their lives to the truth of the gospel;**</u> *<u>to the incarnation and work of redemption revealed in the New Testament Scriptures</u>.* **Instead, they build their lives on all kinds of man-made doctrines and ideas**.

But when I begin to **hear** what Jesus actually says; what God my Father is saying to me through the Son, then I make my commitment and say,

'God I'll put my foundation down right. I'll put my foundation down deep. ***I'll dig past the rubble!*** *I'm not going to build my life on some rubble of human doctrine and tradition; but instead,* ***I'm going to dig right past it all and lay a deep foundation upon the solid rock of the integrity of your Word; upon the integrity of the truth of Your gospel, upon the integrity of Your work of redemption. I'm going to dig down deep, and I am going to lay the foundation of my heart and life, upon the undiluted, unpolluted milk of your Word*** <u>*that I may grow thereby*</u>*.'*

Within that kind of quality relationship I can know for sure that that rock *becomes my strength.*

That means the house now becomes just as sound and strong as the rock that it's built upon. That house has **the same confidence, the same strength** within itself *because of its relationship with that rock.* **That rock *imparts* <u>a strength that is of God</u>.**

I believe it's so important for us if we study the principle of being steadfast in our spirit; *of becoming strong in our inner man* – it's important for us to begin to realize that *that strength doesn't come by accident.*

It doesn't come with time or just kind of one day when we wake up and then suddenly we find ourselves and we're strong.

It comes with a consistent quality relationship with the strength of that rock.

We need to begin to realize **we *can* draw from that rock. We draw from its strength** *when the storms hit.*

Paul says in Ephesians Chapter 6,

*"Having **done all to stand** (...***then go ahead and quit!***)"*

NO!

He says,

"Having done all to stand;"

*"...**stand therefore**..."*

What do I do **to stand**? I mean, **how do I make a stand**?

Most of us, you know, we get the slightest opportunity to fall and we almost say, *'Thank you,'* and there we go, off we go, and we fall and we think, *'Well I have a good excuse.'*

But Paul says,

"Having done all* (everything possible) *to stand, stand therefore*...*"

What does it **take to stand**? **What do you do to stand**?

You don't rely on your own strength. *You draw from the strength of the rock.*

When there are problems in your relationships and people come against you with all kinds of animosity and gossip and accusation and whatever, **you begin to draw from that strength of your Father's love.** *You begin to draw from it and drink from that rock and allow that rock* **to sustain you to be steadfast in your soul, and in the quality of your love walk.**

Streams might break loose against you to destroy you, *to flatten you,* **but you're saying,**

'God I'm standing *in this rock relationship with YOU.* **I'm not going to settle for a weak relationship, for a relationship of self-deception.'**

You see, a relationship of deception is a house that is built upon the sand. The same effort went into building that house. I mean, you know, there's also spiritual effort involved. That person is also going to church and reading the Bible, and doing all those things. *BUT that house falls every time,* **because of an inferior foundation, because of their inferior, weak faith!** *It's a faith that is* **not connected** *to the rock; a faith that* **doesn't draw its strength from the rock.** *The rock is not* **the source of its strength and enablement!**

God wants us to <u>live</u> in holiness. That means *He wants us to live <u>in relationship</u> with Him, He wants us to live <u>in a faith-relationship towards His Word</u>; to be a house that stands and stands and stands.*

He wants us to live in houses and be houses ourselves that are totally storm proof, guaranteed.

That's the security that God and His Word alone guarantees. And I believe that this guarantee includes *every <u>believer.</u>* This security is for *<u>every believer</u>*. This strength is for every Christian; *<u>every</u> true Christian!*

Actually it's for the whole world, amen, *but <u>only the believers</u>,* only the true Christians *fully embrace it and enter into it!*

Faith is within our reach! We are faith compatible! We are Word of God compatible! We were designed for intimate relationship with God! We were designed for a faith-relationship with the Word of God!

Romans 10:17 says,

*"Faith **comes by <u>hearing</u>** (by insight), and **<u>hearing</u>** (that insight comes) by the Word of Christ;* (In other words: Faith comes through insight into the gospel truth as it is revealed in Christ)*."*

As I see you in my imagination, sitting there, reading this book, *I know that every one of you can live in <u>holiness.</u>* Every one of you **can live in <u>intimate relationship with God</u>; in a faith-relationship** with the Word of God, with the truth of the gospel, **with that which is revealed in work of redemption.** Every one of you can live **a steadfast life** in Christ Jesus, **a firm, strong life** in Christ Jesus! **As you gain revelation knowledge, as you gain insight and understanding, as you gain that strength** I know that you will know the blessing of James 1:4,

"To be perfect and complete, lacking nothing."

Then you will always be in a position to overflow in the blessing of God to somebody else. Amen!

Hallelujah!

I really believe that **this is the truth.** I believe that I'm not writing from my top five inches, *but I'm writing* **from the living Word of God, from the very mind of God!**

I really do believe that **<u>a diligence in our hearing and a diligence in our action</u>** *would bring about an intimate relationship with God and His Word.*

In Romans 4:20 we have a beautiful Scripture that recalls Abraham's faith. There was something in Abraham's faith **that relates very specifically to our faith,** *because Abraham*

68

walked in **a very particular, a very specific relationship to** the Word of God that came to him. He walked in a very particular relationship *to the gospel, the good news that came to him, the very promises which he heard from God.*

There was so much that contradicted what God spoke concerning Abraham, what God had to say concerning this man. There were so many things in the natural that said: *"**Impossible!**"* It tried to speak to him and say, *"**It could never be!**"* But never-the-less, the scripture says in verse 19 that,

*"Abraham **grew strong in his faith**."*

Abraham grew strong. He was empowered in his inner man, *in his spirit.*

How?

*"…by **giving glory** to God."*

He began to **focus his attention**, *not on other people's opinions,* but **on God**. And as he focused his attention, his opinion, upon God, *there was a praise, and there was an appreciation - a glory, a glorification in him.* He continued to just give **glory** to God, and it says in verse 20 that,

*"…***he was fully persuaded (he became fully convinced not only that God was able, but)** *that God was going to do what God promised.*"

I believe the *"**fully persuaded**"* has to do with the measure of your steadfastness.

But now, it is one thing *to be fully persuaded* **while you hear the gospel preached,** it's one thing *to be fully persuaded* **while you sit in the gathering of the saints and you feel the anointing of the Spirit, and you feel His presence.** But <u>that full persuasion</u> **wants to take you** *right into the face of the storm.* **It wants to take you** *right into the face of the enemy,* **and** *totally sustain you, right there,* **and eventually** <u>defeat him utterly</u>.

Ha... ha... ha... Hallelujah!

What would be the use of *being fully persuaded* **if it was only something that lasts five minutes after the service, and** *then it's gone, then it's back to double-mindedness again?*

I believe God is bringing His Church back to single-mindedness. He is bringing us back to being a single-minded people, a narrow-minded people who are *fully persuaded; full of faith and power!*

I want to be a narrow-minded person, a single-minded individual, ***with a mind* <u>set</u> *on the THINGS THAT ARE* <u>ABOVE</u>*, where I am seated with Christ in that unseen realm of spirit-reality;* <u>*in that realm of truth and authority*</u>***, in that heavenly realm, the spiritual realm, the realm of reality,*** <u>*far above*</u>***, not just above, but FAR ABOVE,*** <u>***all***</u>

contradicting circumstance and power and might and dominion of the enemy.

*I want a mind **set** on things that are <u>above</u>,* not on the things that are on the earth. *They're not worth thinking about,* amen!

Chapter 6

Being Fully Persuaded

If you will, go with me to Hebrews chapter 10. I want us to look at a few more scriptures *that relate to our relationship with God's Word of Truth; the truth of the gospel.*

Hebrews 10:35,

*"Therefore do not throw away **your confidence**."*

I want you to know that your confidence is <u>you being fully persuaded</u>.

He says, ***"Don't throw it away."*** Why would I **throw away <u>my confidence</u>?**

Obviously because the enemy would draw me into an opportunity *where I **feel** like, 'Well it's not working. My faith is not worth holding onto; I'm not going to do it any longer. I'm not going to try and stand any longer, because I can't figure out how it's going to work out. And oh, this and that, and the other thing, and I've found all the reason I need to just give up and quit.'*

Brother, sister, **God says,** *"****Do not throw away your confidence…****"*

We are dealing with GOD's word here!

DO NOT THROW AWAY YOUR CONFIDENCE!

DO NOT QUIT STANDING! DO NOT GIVE UP BELIEVING!!!

This is God's word *for you* TODAY!

GOD is saying to not quit standing! DO NOT GIVE UP YOUR FAITH!

He, who has ears to hear, let him hear *what the Spirit of the Lord is saying!*

Even if you've had **all the opportunity in the world**, even if you've come to a place in your particular situation, in your particular problem, **to where you now <u>feel</u> like you have enough reason to give up your faith, and to just quit standing.**

DON'T GIVE UP!

DON'T QUIT!

God says,

*"Don't throw away **your confidence!**"*

"BECAUSE YOUR CONFIDENCE HAS GREAT RECOMPENCE OF REWARD!!!"

The reward will only *be released to you* <u>through your confidence,</u> *through your*

confidence in God, through your confidence in you Daddy's love!

It will only be released through your confidence in His word of truth, through your confidence in the integrity of <u>HIS</u> WORD; through your faith!

Your confidence reveals your STEADFASTNESS.

"<u>Let</u> STEADFASTNESS have its <u>full effect</u> so you may be complete, lacking in nothing!"

You see, the full reward is *in your confidence*. **The <u>full reward</u> that God has for you** *is in your confidence.*

The writer of Hebrews continues to say there in Hebrews 10, Verse 39, *"We are not of those <u>who shrink back</u> and are destroyed…"*

God is not the One who threatens to destroy us if we shrink back. NO! But you see, it is the enemy, through circumstances, who wants to destroy us. ***And if we shrink back from faith; if we lose our confidence and allow doubt and double-mindedness and fear to begin to rule our hearts,*** then the enemy has us exactly where he wants us, *and he is free to then plunder, and to steal, kill, and destroy in our lives.*

God doesn't want that for us! He has better things in mind for us than to be destroyed!

The enemy would seek to gain ground against you *at every opportunity*. He would seek **to challenge you every time**, around the next corner and the next corner, and the next one. And you would hear a word from God in this book here today *that blesses your spirit, **and you receive it as The Truth**, but around the next corner **the enemy would challenge you on that Truth again**.*

But Jesus would say to you,

"Give the devil no ground."

That means,

*'Satan, **I'm no longer going to allow or permit you** to exercise your workings and your schemes <u>against my faith</u> in any measure in my life. I permit you <u>no</u> ground. In fact, I'll gain every inch of ground in my life, <u>standing firm in faith</u>. I'll allow God's Word, God's Truth to gain the upper hand; <u>the authority</u> in my life. I'll not be of those that shrink back from faith, but of those who press on in faith; BELIEVING, and TRUSTING all the way!!!!'*

Let's turn the page to Hebrews 11 and let's look at verse 15,

*"If they had been <u>thinking</u> of that land from which they had gone out, **they would have had opportunity to return**."*

I want you to see the principle here that **your mind and your emotions can ensnare you**.

You see; your mind **can trap you** in your past. **Your <u>uncontrolled thinking</u> can give you** *an opportunity to return* back into bondage. I mean, just <u>loose thinking</u>, just <u>casual thinking</u> *could be the very next step into bondage*.

'O, come on now brother Rudi, that's a little fanatical, isn't it? **It's just a casual thought that I kind of permit and entertain. What could be the harm in that?** *I'm not hurting anybody; nobody knows about it but me.'*

Hey listen; *after everything that God has done to deliver you,* **that one seemingly innocent thought, that casual, sinful thought, that weak thought** *you entertain and permit to influence your fickle emotions <u>could take you straight back into bondage</u>. It could take you* **right back into Egypt!**

After everything that God has done to deliver you *it would be like a dog that returns back to its vomit.* Because, remember, the vomit *becomes attractive* to that dog *before he returns to it. He has a twisted picture in his mind* of that meal!

A mind that is not disciplined by the Word would get into trouble *just like that; just as fast!*

All it takes for some is a moment, a thought, a glance, and off you go, back into bondage!

'Oh …those wonderful leeks and the onions… the meat pots of Egypt…'

But God says, *"It is dung. It is refuse! Don't go there!"*

I believe that the renewing of your mind *has everything to do* with a developing of a quality spirit; *a steadfastness in your spirit, a steadfastness in your faith, a strength in your spirit; a consistency in your confidence.* I believe it has everything to do with *BELIEVING and EMBRACING GOD's WORD; GOD's TRUTH!*

And therefore there is a strength built into your inner-man and it begins to speak, just as it is written: *"I believe and therefore I speak"* You too begin to speak from out of your inner-man, from out of that strength and you begin to declare:

*'I will **not** throw away my confidence. **I will not** throw away my confidence. I will **draw from that rock**. **I'll build my life upon it.** I will **believe** in it. **I will believe the Word. I KNOW IT IS TRUE**. I'll <u>put</u> my trust in it to **sustain me**, and **I KNOW IT WILL;** because **God Himself guarantees it;** He is **intimately involved with it**.'*

Listen; **God Himself is enforcing HIS WORD, HIS GOSPEL, HIS TRUTH in the lives of those who become fully persuaded in it; those who put their trust in it!**

So, from that faith of God alive in me, from that new strength, that divine enablement within my spirit I begin to speak and declare: *'I'll **hold fast** to that rock. I will **not** throw away MY CONFIDENCE!!!'*

Hebrews 11:15,

*"If they had been **thinking** of the land from which they had gone out, **they would have had opportunity to return.**"*

Can you now see how it is possible *for any Christian* **to return back into bondage?**

Let's read on.

Hebrews 11:16,

*"But **they desire** a better, even a heavenly country. **Therefore, God is not ashamed to be called their God**, for He has prepared for them a city."*

Who is the *"they"* he is referring to?

Those who have become fully persuaded in the Message, **those who do not throw away their confidence,** ***those who have learned how to discipline their minds through the Word!***

Hebrews 12:1,

*"Therefore **since we are surrounded** by so great a cloud of witnesses…"*

This cloud of witnesses refers to **every** saint, **every believer** that Hebrews 11 makes mention of. These people are not just people that died and now they're gone. God is the God *of the living* and not the dead (Matt. 22:32). **These people make up a great cloud of witnesses**. *Every one of them will testify to the integrity of God's Message.* **Every one of those saints, those believers listed in Hebrews 11 will say to you,**

*'**Don't give up! Don't quit! Don't shrink back from having FAITH! Become fully persuaded in what GOD SAYS in His word and don't throw away your confidence!**'*

Every last one of them! They'd say to you,

*'Hey man, listen, **it's worth every little bit of energy within you to hold on to the promises of God**.'*

Every one of those saints; bar none!

Listen, I'm not interested in a saint who is a failure. *I mean as far as getting that person's opinion.* **I'm not interested in listening to somebody's testimony** *that testifies of failure.* I want to listen to and read the testimony *of them **that overcame**,* and I then, *being encouraged by them,* I want to say,

'**God if they overcame *I too can be an overcomer in this life.***'

I am surrounded, when I read the Scriptures, I am surrounded by a *great* cloud of witnesses, not only in number but **in strength** before God, **because they conquered**,

"...through the blood of the lamb and through the word of their testimony, and because they loved not their lives even unto death."

They conquered!

Chapter 7

Responding Aggressively

Hebrews 12:1–2,

*"Therefore, **since we are surrounded** by so **great** a cloud of **witnesses…"***

*"…<u>let us also</u> **lay aside** <u>every</u> weight and sin which clings so closely;"*

*"…and let us run **with perseverance (steadfastness)** the race that is set before us;"*

*"**looking <u>away</u>** (from these distractions and things that make us weak) unto Jesus…"*

*"…the pioneer **(the One who inspires our faith; the very source of)** and Perfecter of our faith…"*

"Looking <u>away</u>…"

Looking <u>away</u> from the present, **<u>away</u>** from the problems, *unto Jesus*. **Looking away from the strength of the storm <u>unto Jesus</u>, no longer trying to measure the strength or size of the storm**, but *concentrating* **on the strength of the foundation that we're built upon;** *focusing on* **the very Author and Finisher of our faith!**

*"Looking away **unto Jesus;**"*

"…the Author and Perfecter of our faith;"

*"…**who for the joy** that was set before him;"*

"…endured the cross;"

*"…**refusing to be ashamed of what he stood on**…"*

How did Jesus **count (or consider) it all joy**? I mean how did he, as a man about to die, have joy **set** before him?

He counted it (or considered) it all joy, **because he had a guarantee *in the conviction of his heart* that there was indeed joy set before him**.

Where did it come from?

Jesus, as a man, found that joy in his Father's love and in his Father's Word. He held fast to that joy, He held fast to his Father's Word, *steadfast and immovable,* and so there was joy set before him!

He remained in joy, "…*despising the shame…*"

How do you respond to the shame of your circumstances that would challenge you? How do **YOU** respond to it?

Listen; how you respond reveals your spirit.

You would need to *DESPISE* the shame!

Or do you feel all embarrassed, downcast, and downtrodden?

Hey listen; you need to *DESPISE IT!!!*

Jesus, as a man, *despised* the shame **because he focused on God's opinion; He focused on his Father's love for him!**

That's how he held on to his joy!

And listen, because of it He *is* seated, today still; there is a man seated at the right hand of God – Jesus is eternally seated, at the right hand of the throne of God. He *is,* right now, seated at the right hand of the throne of God. He is **seated** there, **secure**, *forever!*

The world thought, *'Hey, what a failure!'* when they saw him hanging naked on that cross. *'Ha…'* the devil laughed and mocked and said to himself, *'What a failure this Jesus is, and He calls himself the Son of God, He calls himself the Savior of the world, ha… what a failure, He could save others… HE COULDN'T EVEN SAVE HIMSELF!'* And so they all mocked and scorned.

But he despised the shame and therefore HE *IS* SEATED on the throne of God with Him. Jesus right now occupies the highest position of authority in the universe! Jesus right now occupies a place in His Father's presence; *the very One that causes Him to be the Ruler and the Conqueror!* And it is that very victory that He lives in, that He *is* in, **that He also wants you to walk in. It's *that very same victory, seated* with Him <u>in that same peace</u>** at the right hand of God, amen?!

Hallelujah!

Ephesians 2:6,

*"And He <u>**raised us up**</u> together with Him;"*

*"…and <u>**made us sit**</u> together with Him in the heavenly realm* (the spiritual realm, the unseen realm of reality, the realm of authority) *in Christ Jesus."*

*"...**complete, lacking nothing!**"*

Hebrews 12:3,

*"<u>**Consider**</u> him* (Jesus) *who endured (**who stood steadfast and immovable** against) <u>such</u> contradiction against him, <u>such</u> hostility from sinners;"*

"…so that <u>you</u> may not grow weary or fainthearted."

He *"endured* **(He stood steadfast and immovable against)** *such contradiction against himself,"*

86

*"…**such contradiction**…"*

And here we thought,

'Well, Jesus had it easy you know, <u>He was special</u>, He was the Son of God, I mean He just did it so easily and that was it.

I mean it is one thing for Jesus to live in victory, but what about me?'

The writer of Hebrews says,

"<u>Consider</u> him… (…the man, not the God… the man)"

Why must I **consider <u>him</u>**?

So I can just think about him as someone who's the only one who ever lived in victory?

NO!

I must **consider him** *so I could draw from that rock.* I must **consider him** *so I could draw from that victory!* I must **consider him** *so I could draw from that foundation to my faith.* I must **consider him** *so that that same strength will become my strength, amen!* **The strength of the rock** *becomes the strength of the* **house***.*

*"Consider him **who endured**…"*

You see that endurance he walked in, even as a man, that steadfastness, was the result of

developing a strong spirit. That strong spirit he developing **caused him to <u>endure</u>**, to last and last and last and last in **the face of <u>every</u> contradiction.**

As a man *who believed God's word and yielded himself fully to the Spirit of Truth, to the Spirit of God,* **he embraced the truth, he embraced what God said,** and so he developed **a strong spirit** and **endured**, *even in relationships*, even against such hostility from sinners.

*"**Consider him** who endured such contradiction against himself, such hostility from sinners,"*

"...so that you may not grow weary or fainthearted..."

Why must I **consider** him?

Just so that I will think, *'Well, Jesus you're wonderful'?* He is wonderful! But, that's not why I must **consider** him! I must **consider** him, **"...so that <u>I</u> will not grow weary and lose heart."**

That means: I must **consider** him *so that <u>I</u> won't become weak-kneed* **and just give up!**

I am talking about considering **the man** Christ Jesus now; *not about the risen Lord!* When He became **a man, *he fully became man;*** He became *100% equal with us in all things,* **even though he was still 100% God; 100% equal**

88

to the Father - the exact representation of His character and of His being; the expressed person of the invisible God, who is LOVE!

Jesus was God *incarnate;* **He fully became a man. He became 100% equal with us in all things.**

Right now, I want you to FULLY realize that when Jesus became flesh; *when he became one with the human race,* **he fully represented us, and he fully shared our humanity; he became like us in every way.**

Otherwise it would be absolutely foolish for the writer of Hebrews to tell us **to consider him.**

I mean why would I bother to consider him if he was not like me in any way, if he was somehow different, if he was somehow special; *if he didn't fully share and represent my humanity?*

But he did, and he does! *He fully shared and represents YOUR humanity!*

And so, **if he was able to develop a strong spirit and was able to endure, even in the midst of such great contradiction from people, and from the enemy, then you and I** *can* **consider him.**

We CAN CONSIDER him and draw strength from him as we CONSIDER his walk, as we CONSIDER how he lived his life,

*"...**so that we will not grow weary and lose heart**"* when we are faced with similar contradictions to our faith, and trials and temptations and testing from people, or from the enemy.

Remember the cloud of witnesses! What are they saying to us all the time?

'Don't give up! Don't quit!'

Do you know what Abraham is saying to you right now, *if he could speak to you in the spirit?*

He would say to you,

'DON'T QUIT!'

Every one of those saints would say to you,

'It's worth it!'

'*...**it's worth it!!** It's worth holding fast to your faith, **DON'T GIVE UP! DON'T QUIT!!**'*

*"...**so that you may not grow weary or fainthearted...**"*

Weariness and faintness have nothing to do with your muscle strength, but **it has everything to do with the strength of your heart;** *the strength of your spirit.*

It's when your spirit becomes weak that everything else becomes weak around you and you become a failure.

He says in Hebrews 12:4 that,

"In your struggle against sin you have not yet resisted to the point of shedding your blood."

That is very strong language.

If I were to write a little commentary on that verse I would say it like this,

'I would rather die than sin! I would rather die than displease God! I would rather die than give up! I would rather die than quit!'

That's the strength of spirit that God wants to inspire within you!

I mean, for many of us the enemy doesn't even have to come with a mighty weapon to attack us. Just a small little weapon, *and off we go, giving in to his deception.* All he has to do is snap his fingers, *and off we go,* **like an obedient little dog, obeying his deception**.

But God says,

'Resist to the point of shedding your blood. You may die, but have that strength in you; have that strength of spirit that says,

'I will not give in to you Satan, I would rather die. I would rather die than give in to temptation. I won't be that stupid to fall for your lies and deception; I would rather die!"

That is it, amen!

'I WOULD RATHER DIE.'

That's the strength that God wants to inspire within us.

God is looking for believers THAT WOULD RATHER DIE than give up.

God is willing to work that into you **if you would only say within yourself,**

'I'll hold on to The Truth. I'll hold on to the Word of God, because of the cloud of witnesses surrounding me. I'll hold on and I'll believe their report. I'll trust IN MY GOD.'

Praise God for Jesus and His cloud of witnesses!

Hebrews 12:12 says,

"Therefore lift up your drooping hands and strengthen your weak knees…"

Isaiah 35:3 says,

"Strengthen the weak hands, and make firm the feeble knees..."

How do I do it?

The answer is in Isaiah 35:4,

"Say to them that are of a fearful heart; 'Be strong, do not fear! Behold your God…"

Chapter 8

God is Able

Hebrews 12:27–28 speaks of *a city, a kingdom, a people "**that cannot be shaken.**"* **It's because they have an unshakable foundation.**

All the scriptures I am giving you are all scriptures relating to your relationship of strength in the truth of the gospel; **your particular individual personal relationship with the Word of God. Nobody else's relationship can bless you as much as your own,** that's why I am giving you all these. Go and read them and study them *for yourself* and ask God to speak to you in the light of this teaching:

Romans 16:25,

*"Now to Him **who is able to strengthen you according to my gospel**, which is the preaching of Jesus Christ, **according to the revelation** which was a secret for long ages.* (**It was preserved** even though it was hidden from Man's view), *BUT IT IS **NOW** DISCLOSED, and through God's holy ministers, by* (insight and revelation into) *the prophetic writings, is **now** made known to all the nations, according to the command of the*

eternal God, **to bring about the obedience OF faith**.*"*

Paul starts of by saying,

"Now to Him **who is able to strengthen you according to my gospel**;*"*

"…which is **the preaching of Jesus Christ.***"*

I thank God for Paul's gospel. Thank God for the way that Paul preached the gospel and taught on Jesus Christ. I thank God for Paul's revelation. *He had a very sober revelation in his spirit of the new creation and of who the believer is in Christ Jesus,* and so he says here in Verse 25,

"…it's this *gospel that will strengthen you."*

Hey listen; **it's not just any Bible talk that will strengthen you!** Don't fool yourself and just listen to some Bible sermons and think that that's going to strengthen you. ***It's only this specific revelation of Paul on the new creation, on redemption realities, on who you are in Christ Jesus that will strengthen your spirit***.

There are a lot of people preaching from the Bible, but man, after half an hour or an hour of them speaking their theories and traditional thinking based on man-made doctrines, philosophies, and legalism, **you still feel and are as weak and confused as you came in – even weaker**.

Spiritually speaking, and maybe even naturally speaking, **that kind of preaching will lull you to sleep and kill you!** But there is a kind of preaching from the Scriptures **that will strengthen your spirit; it will build into your spirit <u>every bit of strength</u>** that you need *to sustain you -* **to be as steadfast as a rock**, or as a mountain that cannot be moved; **a steadfast, firm believer, steadfast in Christ Jesus**

I like Paul's kind of preaching. He says,

"To Him who is able to strengthen you according to my gospel"

Paul says in another place, in Acts 20:32,

*"...I commend you to God **and the Word of His grace** <u>which is able to build you up</u> and give you an inheritance."*

You see, **God can strengthen you, *but He needs the vehicle of the written and spoken Word to instruct your spirit in His Truth,*** and **according to <u>that</u> Word God is able to strengthen you**.

*"...**according to the revelation of the mystery** which was kept secret for long ages..."*

It's according to **the revelation.** It's not just the mere letter that kills, but it is ***the revelation,* which brings life.**

*"...**according to the revelation** which was kept secret for long ages;"*

*"...BUT IT IS **NOW** DISCLOSED;"*

"...and through God's holy ministers;"

"...by the prophetic writings (the insight and revelation contained in the New Covenant);"

*"...is **now made known** to all the nations;"*

"...according to the command of the eternal God;"

*"...**to bring about the obedience OF faith.**"*

Paul only briefly mentions in this scripture that **there is big difference between the Law and faith.** And, without getting into it in too much detail here in this book, based on what Paul taught I suggest to you that **the Law was not really designed to produce obedience.**

Its purpose was to amplify the power of sin; to highlight the fact that it has power. *The Law was introduced **to reveal Sin for what it is in all its ugly effects upon mankind.*** **The Law, therefore, brings death;** *not life.*

The Law, through its system of reward and punishment, *can only produce short-lived obedience,* **limited obedience, and then eventually and ultimately rebellion. Because it stirs up sin.**

Faith, on the other hand, imparts the truth of God. It imparts the love of God, *and therefore, it also imparts the energy to produce unlimited, unrestricted, obedience from the heart.*

***There cannot be a more powerful, more productive force than faith and love.* It will always out-produce the Law**.

You also need to go and study that word *"**now**"* in the New Testament Scriptures. It is one of the most beautiful words in the Bible and *it will bring you into the greatest adventure of your life!*

God has not called you to live in a vacuum, somewhere in-between tomorrow and yesterday, but *right now.* He has called you ***to LIVE <u>right now</u>.***

Chapter 9

We Need Each Other

If you want to become strong in spirit, the second area to develop steadfastness in is *in the area of love and relationships,* with believers and people in general, *but especially with believers.*

I say again: **If you want to become strong in spirit,** *you're going to have to become strong in your relationships;* <u>**strong in love towards people in general, but especially strong in friendship and fellowship with believers**</u>.

First of all, we talked about our relationship with *the Word;* **with God and His TRUTH** – with the truth of the gospel, with the truth as it is revealed in Christ Jesus, in the incarnation and work of redemption. And now I want us to take a look at our love relationship with people in general, *but especially with the believers,* **because the two go hand in hand.**

The strength of our relationship with the believers, as well as the strength of our love towards all people, *will reveal the strength of our spirit.*

These things are the natural outflow of a strong spirit; *of a spirit strengthened in the truth of the gospel, by the Spirit of Truth Himself.*

The enemy knows that if he can bring a weak link in my relationships, making me weak in relationship building, *not seeing it as that important,* **then he could challenge my authority - he could challenge my person;** *the expression of who I really am,* **he could challenge** *my very being,* **he could even challenge** *my walk, my whole walk in God as a Christian,* **because none of us are called** *to walk in isolation.*

Jesus said that the world would come to know Him _by the love we have_.

1 Peter 4:8-11,

"***Above all, <u>hold unfailing your love for one another</u>*** *since 'love covers a multitude of sins.'"* (See also Proverbs 10:12, 1 Corinthians 13:4, and James 5:8–9.)

"...**Practice** *hospitality* **ungrudgingly** *towards one another."* (That means: **Through love become skilled at it**.)

"Like good stewards of the manifold grace of God;" (That grace is **the very expression of God's heart of love**.)

That means: **"*Like good stewards of the many faceted love of God;*"**

"…serve one another with whatever gift each of you might have."

*"In your speaking one to another, **become the mouthpiece of God.** Speak forth the oracles* (the profound utterances; the truth of the gospel, the very Word) *of God* (In other words, **the Truth as revealed in Jesus, the love God has for all people; *the truth of His love*).*"*

"In your ministering one to another, do it with what you have, <u>let God become your source and your abundance</u>. He will enable you,"

"…that in all things God may be glorified by all of us *through Jesus Christ;"*

"…for unto Him belong the glory and lordship (the preeminence) **over everything** *forever and ever. Amen."*

Peter says, *"**Above all**…"*

Do you believe that that's priority number one when the Holy Spirit through Peter says, *"**Above all** …<u>**hold unfailing**</u> your love for one another…"*?

It is one thing to love one another, you know, when *it's just nice to love **and everything <u>feels</u> good.*** But when Ephesians 4:1 *has to come into operation,* I mean, **when I *have to* do everything in my might** *to, "…**preserve** the unity of the spirit **in the bond of peace,**"* in other words, **when I *have to walk in***

***forgiveness**, "...**forbearing** one another **and loving** one another",* **then *THAT LOVE* becomes <u>*a strength*</u> *in my spirit.* It becomes *the very substance* <u>*that makes me what I am*</u>*!* It becomes *the <u>glue</u>, the very <u>bond</u>, that <u>links me</u> to God and to others, and it <u>keeps me</u> steadfast and immovable.*

In other words it becomes impossible for the devil to take me out, **when I <u>walk</u> in love.** But ***THAT LOVE*** I walk in **cannot be a weak thing.**

You see; **the strong love of God *cannot be compared with that compromised, weak thing the world calls love!***

I say again: ***It is one thing to love one another when everything feels good,*** **but God is calling us to walk in the kind of love <u>that will overcome all challenges in our relationships with one another</u>.**

God knows our design. He knows what He has put in us. *He knows* **the kind of love we are capable of** *and therefore He is expecting us* **to do everything we possibly can** *to, "...**preserve the unity of the spirit in the bond of peace**..."* (Ephesians 4:3)

That means I have to walk *in forgiveness, "...* **forbearing with one another, <u>and truly, genuinely, from the heart, loving one another.</u>"** (Ephesians 4:2)

Therefore the Holy Spirit says in 1 Peter 4:8,

*"Above all, **hold <u>unfailing</u>** your love for one another;"*

*"...**since** '**love covers** a multitude of sins..."*

He says, *"...<u>**unfailing**</u>..."*

Let me tell you, love is not keen to listen to the next story; *to the next bit of gossip about someone else,* about somebody else that failed or has fallen through temptation.

'...have you heard about this one, or ...have you heard about that one, or ...have you heard about So and so?'

Let's stop that kind of conversation in our lives and in our fellowship with one another. Let's not discuss *one another's failings,* or talk about somebody else *that fell,* or somebody else *that didn't make it,* **because you see 'Love covers...'**

Love doesn't judge and criticize; <u>it covers</u>.

<u>**Love covers**</u> *a multitude of sins,* because <u>**love's focus**</u> **is on** *the potential of God already placed in someone's spirit, ready to be encouraged and exhibited!*

<u>**Love's focus**</u> **is not** *on their failings!*

<u>**Love's focus**</u> **is to <u>continue to behold Him</u>** *and His workmanship, His perfection within us.*

Love's focus is to continue to behold Him and *His working within us both to will and to do of His good pleasure.*

Love's focus is to continue to behold Him and His working within us and within one another *to awaken and exhibit what He has already placed within us!*

But let's get back to our scripture. He says here in 1 Peter 4:9,

"Practice (become skilled at) *hospitality **ungrudgingly** towards one another."*

You see, there is a **quality** of hospitality that is revealed in this verse. **God is looking for a quality in our hospitality.**

*"…**ungrudgingly**…"*

That means we have to open our homes, *invite people to come and visit, and become skilled at it.*

It is one thing to be hospitable grudgingly; it is another thing to be it *"ungrudgingly."* That's what reveals the strength of your spirit.

I cannot emphasize enough how important it is for you to develop real relationships *in order to become a part of the extended family of God in a genuine way!*

Listen; Satan is always trying to cause division through the breakdown of <u>genuine</u> relationships. If he can get you *unattached and isolated,* he can mess with your stability, slowly weakening you, and keeping you from making progress in the things of God, *and then he can even lead you astray again.*

Remember this, *"…<u>two is better than one and a threefold cord is not easily broken</u>."*

In fact Ecclesiastes 4:9–12 says,

*"<u>Two are better than one</u>, because **they have a good reward for their labor**."*

*"For **if they fall, one will lift up his companion;**"*

*"<u>**But woe to him who is alone when he falls, for he has no one to help him up.**</u>"*

"Again, if two lie down together, ***they will keep warm; but how can one be warm alone?****"*

*"**Though one may be overpowered by another, two can withstand him**."*

"And (three is even better than two) <u>***a threefold cord is not quickly broken***</u>*."*

Jesus said that the world would come to know Him <u>*by the love we have for one another*</u> (and for them, but especially for one another). **Therefore He desires for us** *to* *walk <u>in unity</u>, and <u>together</u>, "...have a good reward for our labor," making a genuine difference in this world we live in.*

Chapter 10

Walking in True Love

As far as it is up to you, walk in love and forgiveness *towards everyone*.

Romans 14:19,

"Let us then <u>pursue</u> what makes for peace and for mutual upbuilding."

*"Let **us** then pursue…"*

In other words,

"…what makes for peace and mutual upbuilding" **will not pursue you, <u>you must pursue it</u>.** There are plenty of things that will pursue you, **but when it comes to these things, *"…the things that makes for peace and mutual upbuilding,"* you must pursue it, *or it will never be yours.***

The devil, *one of those things always pursuing you,* will steal it from you, *if you let him.* **He would love to tamper with your steadfastness, with your peace and with your upbuilding, <u>*but don't let him*</u>. You pursue** *"what makes for peace and mutual upbuilding,"* <u>**and don't let go**</u>**. Hold on to it with STEADFASTNESS. <u>Count it as</u>**

something precious and don't let go, or you *will* lose it, amen?!

The blessing of steadfastness **is something that I must pursue.** To be built up in my inner man **is something that I must pursue. Fellowship with the brethren, the unity of the Spirit, the bond of peace, friendship and relationship,** are things *I must pursue.* **It won't happen automatically.**

Romans 15:1–2,

"We who are strong ought to bear with the failings of the weak and not to please ourselves."

*"Let each one of us please his neighbor for his good **to edify him.**"*

Notice he says, *"...**to edify him;**"* not just to put up with him.

We are not called to just **put up** with one another's weaknesses but, *"to bear with the weak."* Why? **So that we could,** *"edify."* **them.**

The word, *"edify"* means: **TO IMPART STRENGTH.**

In other words, **we are to EDIFY them,** *so we can impart strength to that weak person.*

We EDIFY in order TO IMPART STRENGTH!

So my relationship is always **a relationship of responsibility in love** towards all people, *no matter how naturally-minded and fleshly-minded they are; no matter how full of worldly thinking or full of sin they are - no matter <u>how weak</u> towards sin they are; no matter how <u>WEAK</u>!*

God wants me to **edify** people, to **edify** that person, **and impart strength to them.** He wants me to *build them up* with encouraging words; *with HIS redemption TRUTH, and with* **HIS LOVE.**

Listen; His redemption truth, the truth of His LOVE, *correctly conveyed and gently imparted, will quicken and encourage the most natural and genuine response from their hearts towards God!*

God is looking for *a completely natural response of love from their hearts towards Him* **because they have realized** *through my words* **that He <u>first</u> loved them,** *and cannot stop loving them; that He is <u>in love</u> with them!*

Then there is also our relationship with the believers. You see, we have an even greater responsibility, in love, especially in our relationship with the brethren, *even the weaker ones,* <u>**because of our connection in the Spirit**</u>**.**

That sense of responsibility in friendship and relationship with every person in our

lives, especially with the believers, *comes from God's love that <u>is</u> within us,* **because we <u>are</u> His image and likeness. <u>It is who I am</u>, and <u>who you are</u>! <u>Love is who I am</u>, and <u>love is who you are</u>!**

*A*nd that love I now discover within me says,

'God I'm going to live, not in a relationship of condemnation towards any person,'

'...but I'm going to live, in a relationship of imparting strength to them, if I can,'

'...that is, if I can earn their trust and gain entrance into their hearts, through love,'

'...to have a voice in their life.'

You see, we could so easily *begin to avoid the weak* and say,

'...well, they are just **too weak** for us, we <u>can't</u> fellowship with them;'

'...they're **too weak** to fellowship with.'

But God says,

'Be in fellowship with the weaker ones; be in fellowship with them!'

God wants us <u>to have that sense of responsibility</u> *because of love! Therefore, prefer the brethren. Go out of your way and*

make every effort to be sensitive to them, and to strengthen them!

Listen; God calls every strong saint to fellowship with the weaker ones. It's not the pastor's responsibility alone, amen?!

When Paul was writing Romans Chapter 15, **he was writing it as a letter to the saints; *to the believers,*** and he said,

"They that are strong ought to bear with the weak."

Hey listen: **That's your ministry**. If you know of someone that is a believer *that may be going through a hard time, or worse yet;* ***that is being lured away by the enemy,*** or simply the ones that just have not been making it to the meetings and gatherings of the saints, for whatever reason, **go and see them.**

Not to now go and condemn them and say, *'…where were you when we had our meeting?'* No! Instead, ***make an effort to be sensitive to them,* and go out of your way to go and visit with them. *Minister to them, strengthen them; edify, encourage, and build them up*. *Help them work through, in faith and love,* <u>whatever it is</u> *they are going through.***

Don't join them in their misery, and in their complaining, and their offenses, and their bitterness and unforgiveness and gossip, or <u>whatever it is</u> they are going through;

111

don't join them in that!* But instead, build into them, and draw them back into strength and love and fellowship with you, *and with the rest of the body.

Romans 15:1–6,

"We who are strong ought to bear with the failings of the weak;"

*"...and **not to please ourselves**."*

*"Let each one of us please his neighbor <u>for his good</u> **to edify him;**"*

"For even Christ did not please Himself,"

"...but he lived his life as it is written; '...the reproaches of those who reproached You fell on Me (I removed those reproaches).'

"For whatever was written in former days was written for our instruction..."

Why?

*"...**that by STEADFASTNESS**..."*

*"...<u>**which comes by the encouragement of the Scriptures**</u>,"*

*"...**we might have consolation**."*

He says, "...**we have consolation**." That means **we are comforted and strengthened.**

Notice that **strengthening and steadfastness *comes by the Holy Spirit, directly through the encouragement of the Scriptures.***

"Now may the God of steadfastness…"

You see, **God is involved in this deal;** *He is the Steadfast One!*

"…The steadfast love of the Lord never ceases..."

He is the Unchanging One!

God is not going to give up on you; *so don't you give up on God and quit!*

"Now may the God of all steadfastness and encouragement grant you (by the Spirit of truth; by the Holy Spirit, through the truth of His Word) **to live in such harmony with one another <u>in accord with Christ Jesus;</u>***"*

*"…that **together** you may **with one voice** glorify the God and Father of our Lord Jesus Christ."*

Hallelujah! What a Scripture!

1 Thessalonians 3:12 & 13

"And may the Lord make you (through your fellowship with Him in the truth of the gospel) **<u>increase and abound in love to one another and to all men, just as we do to you;</u>***"*

"...so that He may establish your hearts unblamable..."

That's again a reference to *"being perfect and complete, lacking in nothing."*

You see, that established heart comes from an increase, an abundance of His love, *because of an abundance of revelation from His Word;* insight and understanding into the truth of the gospel - *into God's grace gift to us in Christ Jesus!*

Romans 15:3,

"For even Christ did not please Himself;"

"...but as it is written: 'The reproaches of those who reproach You fell on Me (I took away those reproaches).*'*

Listen; there is more to people than what meets the eye. People are complicated spirit-beings, intricate in design, multi-faceted and very valuable and important to God! Let us take the time to really love them and listen to them, *instead of labeling them and hating them.* Let us be truly compassionate *instead of accusing people in their sin,* just like James the younger brother of Jesus says, *"Be quick to listen, slow to speak, and slow to condemnation."*

***To love and accept a person* does not mean we are to overlook and even condone their sin. But when it comes to really loving**

people and communicating with people who really do not know the gospel, we have to be very sensitive in our communication with them. We cannot start focusing on miss-conduct; on behavior we disapprove of, it will merely offend people, not cure them.

"Speak evil of no-one," says Paul to Titus; *"Instead, s***how perfect courtesy towards everyone – for we ourselves were once ignorant!***"* - Titus 3:2-4

You see, confronting a person about their sin, *especially a stranger,* is like trying to take a dog's favorite bone away while the dog is chewing on it. Of course that dog will growl at you and might even bite you! But instead of focusing on the bone, why don't we rather present the dog with a juicy piece of steak full of real nourishment. That dog will gladly let go of the bone and get focused on eating the steak instead. The bone has lost its attraction and gets let go of and discarded without much fuss!

Listen, people who are empty and deceived love their sin. They are trying to draw some comfort and fulfillment from their sin. Their sin is like that bone; they are self-medicating their empty cravings! That's what addiction is all about! So, sin is a sickness, a cancer; a corroding disease, but sin is all people know, and all they have to draw short lived pleasure from. They are

deceived about it, but they have idolized it, *and to fight with them over it is not going to get you very far in reaching them!*

Of course we know that sin is a lie and deception, but God has not called us to be the sin-police. We are not called to be legalistic fruit-inspectors like the Pharisees were, and emphasize Hell in order to supposedly try and scare them into letting go of their sin.

You can scare people into becoming religious, but you can't scare people into a love affair with God!

If you are trying to get someone to fall in love with you, you go out of your way to notice them and to befriend them through showing interest in them as a person. You spend much time appreciating them as a person; appreciating and communicating their value and worth, especially to you. Your every conversation is spent complimenting them and serenading them.

And let me tell you that is the worst possible time to bring up the subject of rejection or divorce. There is absolutely no need for such things to even be mentioned or brought up in conversation, and certainly no room for any of it to be discussed in any detail!

The topics of Hell, or sin, or rejection, are the worst topics to bring up in discussion with someone you are trying to share the gospel with!

The very word *"gospel"* means: **good news; *not bad news.* Focus on the good news; focus on God's immense unequivocal love for that person!**

God in His love and passion is trying to draw His lost kids into reconciliation through compassion. He is trying to get people to be reconciled to Him; He wants to draw them through cords of love, not scare them away through fear, and chase them away by focusing on their miss-conduct, and harden their heart through talks of wrath and rejection and Hell!

There is no fear in love; but God's perfect love casts out all fear!

Listen, if sin is a sickness or disease, rather than an offence God is hung up on, *then people need a cure, rather than a rebuke!*

The extravagant love of God demonstrated in Christ and revealed in the gospel is that cure!

It is only revelation into the enormous love of God that sets people free!

We are to genuinely love people **in such a tender, yet passionately strong way *that we accurately communicate the intensity of the love of God for every individual.* It is only**

the clear demonstration and impartation of that love that *actually undoes the sin that is destroying their lives.*

We have a responsibility because of love, to be sensitive to them, in order to strengthen them and rescue them out of self-destruct mode; <u>to impart strength to them with the Word,</u> *<u>with the truth of the gospel;</u>* <u>with the truth of the love of God</u>!

This is our responsibility in the love of God, not only towards those who do not know the gospel, *but especially towards those who do know the gospel and share a special bond of friendship and fellowship with us.*

James 5:19–20,

*"Brethren, if anyone among you **wanders from The Truth**, and someone <u>turns him back;</u>"*

*"Let him know that he who <u>turns</u> a sinner **from the error of his way** <u>will save a soul from death</u> and 'cover a multitude of sins.'"*

That does not mean that it is God who is going to kill them. **Sin still has a wage,** amen,

*"…the wages of sin **is death**…"* - Romans 6:23

God is not the author of that death, amen,

*"…death came into the world **through sin!**"*
— Romans 5:12

It is the enemy that comes to steal, kill, and destroy; **not God!**

God is the author of *LIFE!*

Jesus said in John 10:10,

"The thief, (meaning the devil, he is the one who) *comes but to steal, kill and destroy;"*

*"...**but I have come that you might have life more abundantly.***"

What does *"**life more abundantly**"* mean?

Does it mean that we can now sin *even more abundantly* **and call that life?**

No! Life more abundantly means living life to the fullest; living life *free from sin, not free to sin,* because sin comes but to steal kill and destroy! **That is not life more abundantly!** Sin means to miss the mark; **to miss out on life more abundantly!** It's a distortion; and empty pursuit **that does not lead to life more abundantly** ...oh, it may promise life more abundantly, but it's a lie, a deception, **it only leads to greater emptiness, because it comes to steal, kill, and destroy!**

Jesus came to embrace <u>us</u> in our *distortions and resulting dysfunction.*

He came to embrace <u>us</u>; *He did not however come to embrace our dysfunction*.

He did not come to embrace our distorted identities or any other distortions we have identified ourselves with and clung to! He came to embrace <u>us</u>, *and deliver us out of our distorted identities we have inherited through the Fall, and heal us of our dysfunction.*

He came to embrace <u>us</u>, *not our distortions; not our dysfunction!*

To say that Jesus came to embrace our distortions and dysfunction *<u>is to strip the gospel of all its power</u>*.

Jesus came to reveal and restore <u>our original design</u>.

He came to redeem our minds <u>out of darkness</u>.

He came to rescue us <u>out of every distortion</u>; out of <u>every</u> alternate pursuit of fulfillment, out of <u>every</u> alternative lifestyle *that does not line up with His original design of us.*

He came to save us <u>out of self-destruct mode</u>.

Every alternate fulfillment, every alternate identity we pursue, outside of our original design, does not ultimately satisfy, *it only leads to greater emptiness,* and even more of a confused and wounded spirit, *in desperate need of restoration; in desperate need of God's ultimate truth – in desperate need of the truth of God's eternal love for us, in desperate need of the truth of our original design accurately, fully revealed, and totally, fully restored to us, in Jesus Christ.*

God, who is love, made a personal appearance in Jesus Christ, *to demonstrate His eternal love for us and our true value, our worth, to Him.*

He came to reveal that we are His offspring and that we are in His heart; *we are His exclusively.*

He came to reveal that He is in love with us!

He came to reveal that we are custom designed for and absolutely compatible to the Divine nature, *and that we were meant to live and enjoy life in union with Him, according to our original design.*

He came to reveal the truth of our original design, *and thus to rescue our minds out of darkness.*

He came to save us from every alternate identity we have adopted, and every distorted alternative lifestyle we have pursued and clung to, *in our desperation for Him who is genuine true love personified!*

He came to reveal that, He who is love is in love with us! He came to fulfill us with His love and give our heart a home! He came so we might enjoy the depth of an intimate love-affair with Him, *and thereby have the expression of our true identity restored.*

He came to deliver us out of every distortion *and heal us of our dysfunction!*

Now that my friend is the true gospel!

All God ever wanted to do is demonstrate the extent of His love for us, *and thus save us <u>from deception</u>!*

All He ever wanted to do is genuinely thoroughly love us, *and thus heal <u>our dysfunction</u>!*

All God ever wanted to do is love us with all His heart, *and thus save us <u>from ignorance and darkness, and rescue us out of stupidity</u>!*

All He ever wanted to do is satisfy us with His love, with Himself, *and thus save us <u>from deceitful lusts</u>* (harmful, <u>destructive,</u> and therefore wrong passions and desires, *we have yielded to*)!

He loved us enough to come and *rescue us from every distortion, and <u>out of self-destruct mode</u>!*

People who are *not persuaded and strong in God's word of truth;* <u>**settled in the truth of His love**</u>*,* *settled in the truth of the gospel, settled in the truth of a successful redemption,* **get so easily snared and caught up in deceptive dark forces and habits and things,** and they *don't even realize the destruction that comes with those things,* **until it's too late.** But by then they are already trapped in their folly, and that thing has already begun to bear its ugly fruit in their lives; *the ugly fruit of misery, heartache, emptiness, death, and destruction!*

Our sin is like candy-coated poison. We mistake it for candy, but really, it is poison, and we can't discern the difference. We can't get enough; *and yet it is killing us!*

That's why James says that **we who are spiritual,** *we who are strong and established in God's love, and His redemption truth,* **and can see the snare for what it is;** *we should do everything we can to rescue our brothers and sisters who are being deceived!*

Now I remind you that we are not talking about those who do not know the gospel.

We are talking about *those who do know the gospel and share a special bond of friendship and fellowship with us.*

James says that **we who are spiritual,** *we who are strong and established in God's*

love, and His redemption truth, <u>and can see the snare for what it is</u>; we should do everything we can, to rescue our brothers and sisters who are being deceived!

He says,

*"…let him know that he who <u>turns</u> a sinner **from the error of his way <u>will save a soul from death</u>** and 'cover a multitude of sins.'"*

In Galatians 6:1–2, Paul is also talking about our relationship with those we share a close bond of friendship and fellowship with in the gospel, and he states,

*"Brethren, if a man is **overtaken** <u>in any trespass</u>, you who are spiritual, **restore (rescue)** such a one **in a spirit of gentleness;"***

Not in a spirit of judgment and condemnation, *but in a spirit of genuine, gentle love, and more accurate truth.*

*"…considering yourself **lest you also be tempted;"***

*"…**lest you become puffed up in self-righteousness and pride, coming down hard on your brother, judging him too harshly;"***

*"…**restore** such a one **in a spirit of gentleness**…"*

In other words *don't wound your brother's spirit, and put him under self-loathing and rejection and condemnation,* **by being harsh with him.**

*"**Bear** (remove, carry away) one another's burdens, **and so fulfill** the law of Christ."*

The law of Christ *is that word that declares that* **we are partakes of the Divine nature.**

Thus the law of Christ is also called: *The perfect law of liberty, or the law of the new creation; the law of your restored identity as child of God, the law of the image and likeness of God who is love, fully restored within you. Thus it is the very instruction of Christ* **to genuinely love one another.**

*"**Bear** (remove, carry away) one another's burdens, **and so fulfill** the law of Christ."*

Now listen carefully to Paul's words in 2 Corinthians 1:24,

*"**Not that we have dominion over your faith**, but we are fellow workers **for your joy; for by faith you stand**"*

According to Paul in other words, **we have no dominion over one another's faith. We are only helpers of one another's joy.**

So that means that **we are not to try and manipulate and control people with our words, or our faith - to try and force them to**

think and do what is right, *or what we think is right, or what we think they ought to think and believe and do.*

But we are to try and *rescue them* **and** *strengthen* **their faith,** *and edify them* **with the truth of their original design; with the truth concerning redemption realities,** *if they <u>wander from that Truth,</u> or <u>are overtaken in a trespass</u>.*

We are to rescue them with the Word; with the truth of the gospel, *with the truth of* **God's** *love;* with **God's truth, and God's love.**

It is the power of God released through the truth of the gospel that strengthens them and makes them stand; *they do not stand by our faith.*

Listen; *they either stand by their own faith, by God's faith, by the faith which His message, His gospel, inspires in them, or they don't, period.* **It's that simple.**

We can use the truth, and we can quote the scriptures, and *we can give them an accurate representation of the gospel; of the truth of God; of the truth of their original design, and of the love of God, and of their full restoration in Christ Jesus, but we cannot believe for them.*

They either believe, or they don't, *but they cannot stand on our faith.*

You see we can encourage and challenge them, and impart strength to them, but ultimately, *they cannot stand on our faith.* **They can only stand** *on the faith of God. They can only stand* **on their own conclusions and persuasions and convictions in the Truth of God** *which comes to them by revelation; which* **comes to them by the Spirit of God,** *as they accurately hear and embrace for themselves* **the Truth of God.**

Paul continues to say in Colossians 3:12–13,

*"Therefore, as God's **own** chosen people, holy and beloved;"*

*"...**put on** (***your true identity; clothe yourself with the Divine nature, with who you really are** – **put on***) *tender mercies, kindness, humbleness of mind;"*

(Not being self-righteous or thinking too much of yourself; being full of your own opinions)

*"...put on **meekness**;"*

(...being yielded and obedient to the Word of Truth, the truth of the gospel yourself)

*"...clothe yourself with **longsuffering**;"*

(...being willing to suffer mistreatment from people as you work on trying to rescue them from Satan's clutches through the TRUTH of God; through the LOVE of God)*;"*

*"...**bearing** with one another;"*

(...not only putting up with one another's idiosyncrasies or personality differences, **but actually strengthening each other with the Word of Truth; with the truth of God's love,** removing and carrying away one another's burdens)

*"...**and forgiving one another, if anyone has a complaint against another**"*

*"...**even as Christ forgave you;**"*

*"...**so you also must do.**"*

He uses the word *"must,"* only because it's the only authentic life you can possibly live.

Don't allow, *"...any **root** of bitterness to spring up <u>and take root</u>, **for by the trouble it causes it defiles many!**"* - Hebrews 12:15

You see, *a root of **resentment,** a root of **bitterness;** that bitterness and resentment, will bring a weakness into your relationship.*

The author of Hebrews goes on to say,

"See to it that no one **fails to obtain the grace of God.**"

How does any one of us fail to obtain to the grace of God; *or as a better translation would say,* **"fail to enter into the grace of God already given us"**?

*"...**make sure that no root of bitterness and resentment spring up** and cause trouble* (In other words: **Make sure that no unforgiveness, or playing the blame game continues**) *for by it many become defiled..."*

A root of bitterness will challenge your STEADFASTNESS.

A negative attitude of suspicion towards your brother or sister; that focus on miss-conduct, and that resulting resentment and unforgiveness will challenge your STEADFASTNESS!

How do I see to it that this doesn't happen?

Paul says in 2 Corinthians 2:10–11,

*"Anyone whom you forgive I also forgive. **What I have forgiven if I have forgiven anything, it has been for your sake in the presence of Christ;**"*

*"...**to keep Satan from gaining the advantage over us**, for we are not ignorant of his devices."*

Look at that context. He says that **when we forgive** *it is for all our sakes, and it is **for our own sake in particular, to keep Satan from gaining the advantage over any of us**!*

You see, Satan will gain advantage if you focus on miss-conduct; *if there's resentment in your heart.* **If you focus on**

miss-conduct and you walk *lacking forgiveness* in your life, lacking forbearance, <u>the enemy will gain ground against you</u> in your relationships, and in your life, because you refuse to focus on the love of God exclusively and to be the love of God, to be a partaker of the Divine nature. The enemy gains ground against you, <u>because you refuse to live and walk in love</u>!

He says in Verse 7 & 8,

*"**You should rather turn to forgive and comfort** that person;"*

"…or he may be overwhelmed by excessive sorrow."

*"So I beg you to **reaffirm your love for him**."*

Do you see here the heart of Paul?

He **walked *in such a revelation*** of **righteousness. He walked *in a revelation* of intimate relationship restored with God <u>and others</u> *through the work of redemption.***

He saw *the value* of cultivating true loving friendships, and staying *in fellowship* with the brethren around the truth of the gospel, around the love of God exclusively, and of being part *of a local church; a local body of believers*.

He says here,

"...rather turn and forgive."

RATHER FORGIVE!

Don't let** the enemy gain ground **so that he could root down resentment in your life and defile many.

You see he works **like weeds that begin to grow and begin to choke out the truth of the Word and then begin to bring a distance in your relationship, so he can isolate you, or find a hook in your life, by which he can latch on to you, *to defeat you and destroy you!***

The consistency of your love and forgiveness in your relationships *will bring a steadfastness into your life,* a certain *distinct quality* in your life; *life more abundantly!*

I praise God that we can *lean on* one another; that we can *find a fortress* in one another and *be secure* in one another, convinced that we, together, *with one voice,* glorify Jesus!

And in that glory, *you become my concern* and I become *your concern, and so, mutually we edify one another, and build one another up.*

That's what the body of Christ is all about; becoming <u>real</u> family to one another, because we realize that <u>we already are</u>!

We are the very family *and household* of God; being *loved ones* of God, and of one another!

Together enjoying *life more abundantly!*

Paul continues in Ephesians 4:32, *"**And be kind to one another, tenderhearted, forgiving one another;**"*

*"…**just as God in Christ also forgave you.**"*

In Matthew 18:21–35, we find another very interesting scripture along these same lines:

"Then Peter came to Jesus and said;"

"How often shall my brother sin against me, and I forgive him?"

"Up to seven times?"

*"Jesus said to him, 'I do not say to you, up to seven times, **but rather seventy times seven**.'*

*"**Therefore**…* (Let me tell you a parable to explain what I mean, because I really want you to get the point)

*"…the Kingdom of Heaven **is like**…"*

Listen, you might as well get this straight in your mind, before we even start: **He was not trying to tell them that this is the way God**

our Father is; *that was not the topic of conversation.*

Within their limited sphere of fleshly examples, this is the best one He could employ at the time to try and show them that, **besides hurting the other person,** *you are trying to punish and destroy for offended you,* **you are actually hurting yourself when you won't forgive.**

He was trying to show them how, *when you won't forgive,* **how you always end up eating the fruit of your own unforgiveness, and how that fruit of unforgiveness almost always ends up destroying you.**

So He said:

"...the Kingdom of Heaven **is like** *a certain king who wanted to settle accounts with his servants."*

"And when he had begun to settle accounts, one was brought to him who owed him ten thousand talents."

"But as he was not able to pay, his master commanded that he be sold, with his wife and children and all that he had, and that payment be made."

"The servant, therefore, fell down before him, saying, **'Master, have patience with me, and I will pay you all.**'"

*"Then the master of that servant **was moved with compassion, <u>released the man, and forgave him the debt.</u>**"*

*"But that servant **went out and found one of his fellow servants who owed him a hundred denarii;**"*

(That is a fairly large amount, like 3 month's salary, but still a very miniscule amount in comparison to ten thousand talents)

"…and he laid hands on him and grabbed him by the throat, saying, 'Pay me what you owe!'

Why did he do that?

I believe it was because he still believed he deserved judgment, *even though the king showed him kindness,* and he believed that, just as he still deserved judgment, in all fairness, *so did everyone else! And he wanted to still find a way to somehow justify himself before the king, through his own efforts. In his pride he still wanted to pay the master back,* even if it was in installments, even if the first installment was only 3 months' worth of salary for the average man.

His problem was that *he still couldn't accept forgiveness, and forgive himself, and let go of it,* and therefore he was going to help the king hold everyone else responsible too.

It was a pride thing.

In fact, he might have still been upset, because he got singled out, *or so he felt,* <u>and now he was bitter</u> **towards God and the whole world, because if he deserves judgment,** *then so do they!* **After all,** *'It's what's fair!'*

You see, *if you begin to think that that is the way your King still looks at you,* **then you are going to feel justified** *in looking at others that same way!*

"So his fellow servant fell down at his feet and begged him, saying, 'Have patience with me, and I will pay you all.'

*"**And he would not,** but went and threw him **into prison** till he should pay the debt."*

"So when his fellow servants saw what had been done, they were very grieved, and came and told their master all that had been done."

"Then this king and master, after he had called the man, said to him, 'You wicked servant! <u>**I forgave you all that debt**</u> *because you begged me."*

*"**Should you not also have had compassion and mercy on your fellow servant,** <u>**just as I had pity on you**</u>**?'***

*"**And his master the king was angry. He delivered the man up to the tormentors** (torturers) *until he should pay* <u>all that was due</u>."*

Even until recently, I use to read this portion of Scripture and think,

'Well there you have it, **the King (meaning God)** *got so angry that He revoked His forgiveness, and this man is now going to be delivered up to the tormenters, by God Himself, to be tortured forever in Hell.'*

But there has always been something, *and it has to do with love,* which bothered me whenever I read this Scripture. *It never quite made sense to me in my spirit.* These questions kept nagging at me. For instance, **why throw a man in prison *if you want him to repay his debt*?** I mean, **if a man is in prison, how is he going to be able to work and repay the debt?** And *what on earth is torturing the man going to accomplish?* I mean, **torturing the man is not going to get the debt paid.** Only putting the man to work is going to get your money back, **if you really want your money back, that is.**

So, recently, as I was praying for insight, and while I was reading this scripture, **the Holy Spirit opened my eyes to something I had never seen before.** He began to break open *new revelation* in my spirit and showed me that *there is so much more that the Father is trying to communicate to my spirit than what the casual observer can see.* **He began to reveal to me *the heart of our Daddy God.* He began to talk to me about "<u>all that was due</u>".**

So, let me ask you the same question He asked me: **How much was due**?

The answer is: **NOTHING!**

Why?

Because when his master forgave him the debt, <u>he forgave it all</u>.

So really, if you think of it, *the king wanted this man to grasp something.* He didn't really want to torture the man.

What the Lord Jesus was saying through this parable was that, **the one who refused to let go of judgment, the one who refused to forgive himself and others, was going to be tormented *by his own self-judgment until he was willing to accept his forgiveness* and then he would be able *to release others from their debt as well.***

Only then could he say to the tormenters, *to those legalistic, judgmental demons of accusation and condemnation,*

'Listen guys, you can stop tormenting me now, because **the debt was cancelled. I was completely forgiven the debt,** *and therefore I have* **a legal right to go free** *without suffering any more mental or physical torment, or torment of any other kind.'*

And they would have to let him go, *because he was legally <u>a free man</u>*!

It is interesting to note that the king, in this story example Jesus used, *was very disappointed*. But even though *he got upset in his disappointment,* he never did say, *'I revoke my forgiveness.'*

Another thing that is also interesting to take note of is that *the king did not go and release the other man who was thrown in prison.* ***It was up to this servant number one to accept his own forgiveness, and then to go and forgive his brother, and let him out of prison too!***

Matthew 18:35,

'So My heavenly Father also will do to you'

He will be rightly disappointed with you as His kids, because that attitude and behavior is the furthest thing *from the Divine nature, and from your true self; from your true nature, your original authentic design.*

That is not how the Father's kids ought to act!

He wants us to forgive from the heart *because we are love!* He wants us to forgive *because we are born of Him* and we have learned from Him!

"I forgave you all that debt…"

"Should you not also have had compassion and mercy on your fellow human being; <u>just as I had pity on you</u>?"

'So My heavenly Father also will do to you..."'

He will leave you to the torment **you bring on yourself,** *"if each of you, <u>from his heart</u> does not forgive his brother his trespasses."*

Sin still pays its own wage!

God gave all of us a sensitive conscience, *and your conscience* **will be tormented** *in self-righteousness* (**while trying to be justified by the merits of your own efforts**), *because you will always stand guilty and accused <u>when you do not receive the truth that judgment is over</u>, and that* **on that basis,** *<u>you have been forgiven your debt</u>.* **But more than that, on the basis of the love of God, <u>you have been forgiven your debt</u>!**

Listen; you cannot <u>both</u> owe a debt *and have the debt be forgiven* <u>**at the same time**</u>**!**

Either you owe the debt, *or you don't!*

Either the debt is forgiven, *or it's not!*

Which is it?

It cannot be <u>both</u>!

And we do not just have our debt forgiven, <u>Jesus paid it in full.</u> And not only ours, but that of the whole world, past, present, and future!

You see, *a self-righteous, legalistic attitude and approach,* <u>not God</u>, *will torment your conscience.* And that sin of self-righteousness and religious legalism will mar your blameless, innocent, fellowship with God. It will place you under your own judgment; *a judgment of your own making.* You place yourself under judgment. That judgement you judge yourself with will rob you and *keep you from enjoying true intimacy* in your fellowship with your Father. *It will keep you outside, in outer darkness, TRAPPED.* It will prevent you from experiencing *total, complete, intimacy* with Him. It will keep you from *enjoying* righteousness.

It is *the furthest thing from innocence!*

You will suddenly notice that there is something missing; *that you lost something between you and God* in your personal private times with Him, *and the intimacy you experience is not as deep as it used to be,* as you try to fellowship with Him. You will find *a separation from* your Father's sweet fellowship, *and you will be tormented and suffer this way, until you let go* of your sin of self-righteous

judgmentalism, and religious legalism, *and release your brother from his guilt.*

Jesus said this in Matthew 6:14 & 15, *"For if you forgive men their trespasses, your heavenly Father will also forgive you."*

"But if you do not forgive men their trespasses, **neither will your Father forgive your trespasses***."*

It's not that *He is judging you and* <u>*does not want to*</u> *let go of it.*

No!

He <u>*cannot*</u> *let go of it,* <u>*it is not up to Him*</u>, <u>*It is up to you*</u> **to let go of your trespasses; of your self-righteousness - to let go of unforgiveness.** *It's not up to Him to forgive* <u>*again*</u>**, it is up to you** <u>to receive forgiveness</u>**, to embrace the forgiveness already given to us all in Christ Jesus, and to** <u>let go of judgment all together</u>**!**

He settled the issue of forgiveness forever in Christ Jesus!

We all stand forgiven of our trespasses already!

So it is not a matter of Him forgiving or not forgiving; it's a matter of <u>us letting go</u> **of the judgment, and torment, and accusation, and unforgiveness** <u>ourselves</u>**!**

Of course, He is *not far* from anyone of us!

He is right there; He is near unto us, within us, *to help give us the breakthrough!*

As we lean on Him for help, *breakthrough is not only possible, but <u>inevitable</u>!*

Chapter 11

Called to a Higher Standard

2 Peter 3:17 says,

"You therefore beloved, knowing this beforehand (this should be common knowledge to you)*, **beware, lest you be carried away by the error** of lawless people, **and lose your own stability;"***

*"…but **grow in the grace and in the knowledge** of our Lord Jesus Christ."*

"Lawless people" speaks of men or women **who are not under the government of God's Word.** They're lawless. That means **the Word of God doesn't have any direct influence upon them**. Peter says **to not be co-mingled with them, because they could carry you away into error. *They are not founded upon the immovable Word; the word of a successful redemption, and of righteousness and of the new creation - the word concerning our sonship fully restored in Jesus Christ; of us being partakers of the Divine nature!***

He says that ***they are not founded upon that immovable Word,*** but instead **they are**

tossed to and fro by every wind of doctrine that comes around.

He says, *if you listen to them;* if you hang out with them and become friends with them and listen to them, and allow them to influence you with their way of thinking about life, and their way of seeing things when it comes to God and to truth and to who we are; our identity, they will cause you to lose your own stability.

"...but *grow in the grace and in the knowledge* of our Lord Jesus Christ."

Clearly the growth in His grace and in the knowledge of Jesus *will strengthen my spirit, to be steadfast and not to lose my own stability, but maintain it*.

Proverbs 13:20,

*"He who walks with wise men **becomes wise**, but the companion of fools **will suffer harm**."*

He says,

*"He who walks with wise men **becomes wise**."*

There is something that will rub off on your spirit where you fellowship. I am telling you now, it's the truth!

Where are you in fellowship?

Who are you in fellowship with?

What are you in fellowship with?

The very word **fellowship** implies this: *No matter what you do, because of your fellowship,* **because of your close association with** *it, or with them,* **you will be rubbed off on. No matter what you do they will rub off on you, because you are in FELLOWSHIP with them!**

*"…but the **companion** of fools **suffer harm.**"*

Do not seek the **companionship** of fools! Fools are obviously the opposite of wise people.

Wise people dig deep and lay their foundation *upon the enlightened revelation of Jesus* **as Paul preached about Him.**

Do not walk in the companionship of fools! Fools are people *who are not walking according to the enlightenment of the revelation of Jesus;* **of His work of redemption**.

There are certain **friendships** that you and I must **avoid** within this world.

I'm not talking about isolating myself *and saying, 'I'm not going to connect and minister to them.'* No, I'm not saying that! But so often we say **I'm just going to go and minister** *to my old friends, my natural-minded, worldly friends.* Or, **I'm just going to stay where I'm at and try to minister** to my unenlightened

145

friends, *even though I know they are just busy with religious rituals and customs; even though I know they live compromised lives;* **even though spiritually speaking** *we are unequally yoked.* **In the meantime, it's really just an excuse** *to compromise with them!*

I want you to know that, *even though Jesus sometimes ate with the Pharisees and the Sadducees, and even though Jesus sometimes ate with the prostitutes and drunkards,* **He didn't live a life of compromise** **with any of them!**

He spent time with them *for one purpose:* **to save them;** *to rescue them!*

It was *the compassion of God* **that brought His ministry to them.**

There is **a companionship** *that we need to break with,* *with Man-made religion, and with this world,* **and we need to begin** *to be selective* <u>in our fellowship</u>.

I am determined; I have made my mind up, *'God I am going to FELLOWSHIP with Word-based people, with TRUTH-based people,* <u>*who understand Your work of redemption FULLY*</u>*. I'm not going to FELLOWSHIP with people who are lawless, Word-less people, but with people who are FULL of your Word, FULL of You TRUTH! For in that FELLOWSHIP there's a communication of every good thing that promotes the knowledge of Christ Jesus!*

And within that FELLOWSHIP, Father, *I'm strengthened, I'm edified, I'm brought into STEADFASTNESS, by Your mighty power at work in me, my God!'*

Amen! Hallelujah!

I can guarantee you that **when you begin to *neglect* your relationship with the body of Christ, with the Word-of-truth-based people of God; with believers in the New Covenant, believers in new creation realities, *you will begin to become unstable!***

The moment you begin to just *drift* and do your own little thing, <u>you lose your own stability</u> and you begin to *drift into error.*

But God calls you back into *FELLOWSHIP!*

God says, *"Strengthen the weak hands."* Take a firm hold again; stir up your love again for that FELLOWSHIP; <u>hold onto Jesus, *and His body of believers*</u>.

1 John 1:7 says,

*"If we walk in <u>the light</u> **as He is in the light,*** (if we walk in that same light; *His light,* **agreeing with His truth,** *walking in the same light He is walking in,* **seeing eye to eye with His Word, with His work of redemption,** then) *we* (genuinely, automatically, from a heart full of new creation realities - **from a heart full of God's truth and love**) *we* (genuinely, automatically) ***have fellowship with one***

another, and the blood of Jesus Christ His Son cleanses us from all sin."

It's the abiding word *that inspires* **and sustains** **our love and fellowship with one another.**

1 Corinthians 15:33–34,

*"Do not be deceived: '**Bad company ruins good standards.**'"*

***"Come to your right mind and sin no more.** I do not speak this to shame you, **for some do not have this knowledge of God.**"*

Another translation says,

*"**Awake** unto your righteousness and sin no more."*

The fact that we have received a righteous nature from God *is the knowledge that some do not have* and the very reason why they are still hanging out with bad company *and living in sin.*

***"Come to your right mind** and sin no more..."*

What a strong word of exhortation!

What kind of sin?

I mean what was this sin *linked to?*

"Bad company."

In other words, *friends **who are not worth** *your friendship and companionship,* because they **would ruin** *the very quality God is building **into your spirit and into your life** through the truth of the gospel.* **The enemy would use them** *to rob you and destroy* **that beautiful thing <u>God is building</u> within you**.

1 Corinthians 5:9–13,

"Now I wrote to you in my letter not to associate with immoral people;"

That is people that do not cling to the Word of Truth as their standard; as their source of life.

*"…not at all meaning the sexually and otherwise immoral of this world, or the greedy, and robbers or idolaters, **since then you would need to go out of this world altogether;**"*

*"…but rather **I wrote to you not to associate with anyone who bears the name of brother,** if he is guilty of immorality, sexual or otherwise, or if he is guilty of greed, or if he is an idolater, reviler, drunkard, or a robber and extortioner;"*

(He is talking about someone who is stealing and doing other hurtful things, being underhanded and trying to cover it up, twisting the truth),

*…my instruction is: "…**not even to eat** (to just hang out) **with such a one.**"*

"For what have I to do with judging outsiders? Are not those, within your fellowship of believers, whom you ought to judge?"

*"God judges those who are outside our fellowship of believers, but concerning those who are within I say to you, therefore, '**Drive out the wicked person from among you**.'"*

Now this **may seem** *too* **harsh**, and it **may seem to contradict** what I have been teaching all along *about bearing with the weak and walking in love,* but I believe these wicked ones Paul is talking about, are **people who play games,** *and try to deceive us;* **people** *who pretend at first* **to want to change, and to want to have** *a genuine relationship* **with God,** *but they really don't.* **They have no intention of embracing what we believe and hold dear;** **they are merely trying** *to pull the wool over our eyes.* They are **people who** *persist* **in wickedness, and** *refuse* **to listen to exhortation, and are really** *un-repentant of their sin,* **even though they** *try to pretend* **when they are with us. They are deceptive and** *hard of heart,* **and secretly, or some even openly,** *refuse to listen* **to someone who tries to draw them away from their sin** *and into real love and fellowship with God and the believers.*

The words, *"do not associate"* – SUNANAMINOSTA in the original Greek – means: **not to mingle or associate *intimately*.**

Listen, God says that ultimately you cannot maintain <u>intimate fellowship</u> *with one who lives a hypocritical life;* one who bears the name brother, and says, *'I have fellowship with God,'* <u>but he lies; he *walks in darkness*</u>.

Psalm 119:130,

"The entrance of Your Word brings light."

God says in 1John 1 that the quality of our fellowship is measured by *the light, and that light is the Word of God;* ***the Word of Truth, the gospel of our salvation and glorification established in Christ and His successful work of redemption.***

Our fellowship is built upon **The Truth** *as it is revealed in Christ; as it is revealed in the gospel, and communicated in the scriptures.*

We relate to one another *through the New Covenant;* **through** *New Creation Realities!*

Proverbs 27:5–6 says,

*"**Better is an open rebuke** than hidden love."*

*"Faithful are **the wounds** of **a friend;** but even the kisses* (or flattering) *of an enemy is deceitful."*

He says,

*"**Faithful are the wounds** (or blows – the chastisement) **of a friend.**"*

He says,

*"**Better is open rebuke than hidden love**…"*

A couple of times in my life so far I've had to speak very **straight** with some individuals. Both times they were offended and accused me, saying, *'You are no longer walking **in love**, brother, you say you love us; **but you don't! You wouldn't be intruding in our private lives if you did!**'*

But I kept on insisting that it was *because of my strong love for them* **that I felt compelled to speak this straight with them. I made sure, in love, *to be very gentle,* as I said what I had to say!** The one person just continued to harden their heart, but in my dealing with the other person, the Holy Spirit quickened this exact scripture to me, and I read it to them, *and they broke down and wept.* **They were set free and restored *and brought back into health and strength and true fellowship* with God.**

*"**Faithful are the wounds of a friend**, but the kisses* (or flattering) *of an enemy is **deceitful**."*

**You see, true love *is a <u>strong</u> thing.* It's not a *weak,* wishy-washy thing. The love of the New Covenant *does not excuse sin; but deals with it <u>in love</u>*. It wounds very gently. *It's a wound <u>that brings healing</u>.* It's like doing a necessary surgery. Sometimes it still hurts, it is still a wound, *no matter how much you try not to hurt and wound them,*

but it is for their good; it brings ultimate healing! It helps them; it saves their life!

The love of the New Covenant, the love of God; *that true genuine love awakened in our hearts by the Holy Spirit, doesn't say,*

'…well, brother it doesn't matter, we'll fellowship with you, ***you can carry on living in fornication and adultery, or homosexuality, or some other kind of distortion, like lying and cheating and manipulation and embezzlement of funds, or doing your drugs, or whatever it is you are accustomed to, or addicted to doing;*** *you can carry on doing your stinky business, because we'll just continue to cover that sin,* ***as long as you don't really hurt anyone else too much, or draw too much attention to yourself.'***

NO! That is not what this love of God that is awakened in our hearts says!

That's not what this true love says!

This love *will love you enough to even be an open rebuke* and say,

'…brother if you continue that way it will lead surely to death in every way, ***but I love you beyond that; I will love you beyond your transgression; I will love you right out of your transgression! You can be set free and totally released from that thing today, by the power of God, as I lay hands on you and pray for you, <u>if you would only receive</u>***

it! I want to love you and see you forgiven and released and restored right back into true fellowship with us and the Father and with His Son and with the Holy Spirit.'

"...open rebuke..."

It is genuine love in action!

*"...speaking the truth **being saturated with love!**"*

There is another scripture in Proverbs 20:30 that talks about this:

"Blows that wound cleanse away evil;"

"Wounds make clean the innermost depths of the heart."

You see *"open rebuke"* **could wound you, but it's a wound that will bring healing.**

That doctor's knife wounds your body *to remove that root of cancer, or to remove that deep-seated root of bitterness.* **It's a wound that saves your life! It's a wound that brings healing, amen!**

Hallelujah! Thank you Jesus!

You would do well to go and read 1 Corinthians 13. The whole chapter is about **seeing yourself clearly, AS IN A MIRROR, *your true self; the one who is the image and likeness of God.* That entire chapter relates to**

walking in love, _because that is who you are_!

Don't do window-shopping when you read it, thinking that you can never become like that and that the best you can hope for is that this is what we will be like one day in Heaven.

NO!

This is who you are, _right now, already_!

Love is who you <u>are</u>, not who you're going to become someday.

Remember: YOU **ARE** A <u>NEW</u> CREATION **_NOW_**!

Romans 12:1 & 2,

"I beseech you therefore brethren, by (in view of) _the mercies of God, that you present **your bodies** a living sacrifice, holy, acceptable to God, which is your **reasonable** service."_

It is only logical; _not unreasonable at all._ **It's the only authentic life you can live.**

"...And do not be **conformed**..."

(That means to be pressured into a mold, shaped, manipulated into inaccurate, wrong, thinking; manipulated _into being something you are not_)

*"...And do not be conformed **to this world*** (and the way they think. **They believe a lie about themselves;** *they are self-deceived*),

*"...but be **transformed**..."*

He is referring to the process of metamorphosis by which a caterpillar is changed into a butterfly.

Listen; that caterpillar was always meant to become a butterfly. In fact, *that caterpillar always was and is a butterfly; **its true nature comes forth in the metamorphosis***.

James 1:18,

*"...**Of His own will He brought us forth** by the Word of TRUTH..."*

We, too, believed The Truth and were "*brought forth*" by it.

John 8:36,

*"...Whom the Son **sets free** is free indeed."*

Romans 12:2,

"...And do not be conformed to this world, but **be transformed *by the renewing of your mind***, *that you may prove* (taste and experience for yourself) *what is the good, acceptable and perfect will of God."*

*"...**Be transformed <u>by the renewing of your mind</u>,** that you may **prove,**"* not just taste and experience for yourself, *but also to show forth through your life to the world, "...what the will of God is."* So that through encountering your life God's will may become *"good, acceptable and perfect"* to them also.

You see, we are to *genuinely love people in such a way that we help set them free* from the sin that is destroying their lives.

In other words, **our love needs to be pure *and we need to do everything we possibly can* to rescue them with the Word, with the gospel, with the truth and love of God; *with the truth of redemption and restoration accomplished in Christ Jesus - with the truth of the love of God their Father, their true Daddy, <u>for them</u>!***

So, if you want to develop steadfastness in your spirit, if you want to develop a strong spirit, then you need first of all to check up on your relationship with the Word of God, with the truth of the gospel; with redemption realities, with new creation realities.

How diligent are you in your hearing and how diligent are you in your doing?

And then we have also talked about walking in love in our relationships with one another, and with all other people.

But Acts 9:20–22 also speaks of another quality. **If you want to grow strong in your spirit, *then you must become bold in that strong love;* strong and bold in your conviction of God's truth and love,** and do what Paul did.

Acts 9:20–22,

"And immediately in the synagogues he proclaimed Jesus, that He is the Son of God."

"Then all who heard were amazed, and said, 'Is not this the man who made havoc in Jerusalem, and destroyed those who called on this Name, and he has come here also for this purpose to bring them bound before the chief priests?'

"But Paul increased all the more in strength *and confounded the Jews who dwelt in Damascus,* ***proving that this Jesus is the Christ."***

Notice what he did: *"And in the synagogues **<u>immediately</u>** he proclaimed Jesus."*

This is immediately after his conversion; *immediately after making the decision to embrace Jesus Christ fully, to embrace this God of love, his true Father, and to follow the truth as it is revealed by the Father, so clearly, in Jesus.*

So, immediately after faith was birthed in his heart, *he began to publicly proclaim Jesus and the success of His work of redemption!*

If you want to increase in spirit-strength, *begin to proclaim immediately the One you believe in. Proclaim this One you love; this One who saved you by His grace in that successful work of redemption.*

Don't be a silent witness!

Begin to immediately proclaim *and you'll increase* **and you'll begin to profound both Jews and Greeks** *with the integrity of the love of God, and with the integrity of the Word of the New Covenant; the integrity of the truth of redemption!*

That means you'll begin to confound both believers and unbelievers alike *who do not have The Truth of the Gospel, and are therefore living compromised lives.*

Father, we have no excuse before you to be weaklings, *but we have the same Spirit of Faith and Truth* as he had who wrote, *"I believe and so I speak."*

Father, **we also** *believe,* **and therefore <u>we speak</u>!**

Father your Word says that even though **we may be afflicted in many ways,** *yet we are* *not crushed.* **We may be persecuted for our strong stand;** *but we are not in despair!*

I thank you Lord God that **this is the victory that overcomes the world,** *even our FAITH!*

And Father, **You've placed this strength, this strong faith** *within us,* **to be more than conquerors** *in <u>this</u> world!*

And You blessed us with *this* revelation and *this* knowledge of Your Word; of *this* gospel, and of Your LOVE *for us* and for all people, **so we could be a blessing** to one another, **as we daily consider** *how to stir up one another,* **and encourage one another,** *to be strong, and remain strong in the Lord and in the power of His might;* **walking in the love and good works** *you designed us for,*

…**and touch with Your love our fellow man,** *and help them with Your TRUTH;*

So we could say to those who have fainted and grown weary, Father, *to* **wake up** *and to* **wait upon** the Lord; **to intertwine themselves with You,** *and to grow strong in You*, <u>*and to take courage;*</u> **to mount up again** as of with wings of eagles, **and soar with You** <u>*above*</u> **all** *contradiction that comes their way in life!*

Hallelujah!

Father, we can truly say to them: **Don't give up! Don't Quit! Develop a strong inner self! You <u>can</u> do it! It is your inheritance!**

Father, we want to be that people of strength; those strong saints *full of truth wrapped up in love!*

...those strong saints *full of <u>Your love</u>!*

...that people of strength *that You <u>desire</u>!*

Thank you for the truth of Your gospel; *the strength of Your love towards us!*

Thank you Holy Spirit, *for ministering strength to the readers of this book.*

Strengthen them *with might* in their inner man, Lord; You are so good at that!

Right now by faith, *I release Your strength to them in their spirits;* the strength *of your love, and of Your truth;* the strength *of Your faith!*

Thank you Father God.

Amen.

In closing, I urge you to get yourself a copy of *The Mirror Bible.* It is the best paraphrased translation of the Scriptures from the original Greek that I have ever read, because it reveals God's heart and Paul's gospel the clearest. It's available online at www.Amazon.com and several other book sellers.

If you want me or someone from of our team to come to where you are, *anywhere in the world,* and give a talk, or teach you and some of your friends *about the gospel message and these redemption realities,* simply contact us at www.LivingWordIntl.com, or you can always find me on Facebook.

If your life has changed as a result of reading this book, *please write to me and let me know.*

I would love to share in your joy *so that my joy in writing this book may be full!*

"That which was from the beginning, which we have heard **(with our spiritual ears)**, which we have seen **(with our spiritual eyes)**, which we have looked upon **(beheld, focused our attention upon)**, and which our hands have also handled **(which we have also experienced)**, concerning **the Word of life**, we declare to you,

that you also may have this fellowship with us;

and truly our fellowship is with the Father
and with His Son Jesus Christ.

And these things we write to you
that your joy may be full."

- 1 John 1:1-4

About the Author

Rudi & Carmen Louw together oversee: Living Word International.

They also travel and minister both locally and internationally.

Rudi was born and raised in the country of South Africa, while Carmen grew up in Cortland, New York.

They function in the ministry of reconciliation (2 Corinthians 5:18-21) and flow strongly with the Holy Spirit and His anointing to teach, preach, prophesy, heal, and whatever is needed to touch people's lives with the reality of God's love and power.

God has given them keen insight into what He has to say to mankind in the work of redemption concerning the revelation and restoration of humanity's true identity.

Therefore they emphasize THE GOSPEL, IN CHRIST REALITIES, the GRACE of God, the WORD OF RIGHTEOUSNESS, *and all such eternal truths essential to salvation and living the CHRIST-LIFE.*

They have been granted this wisdom and revelation into the knowledge of God by the Spirit of Truth; that resurrected Spirit of Jesus Christ, *to establish and strengthen believers in the faith of God, and to activate them in ministering to others.*

Not only are people set free from the poison and bondage of sin, condemnation and all kinds of intimidation, (upheld, strengthened and reinforced by age old religious ideas born out of ignorance) **but many are brought into a closer more intimate relationship with Father God, as Daddy**, through accurate teaching and unveiling of the gospel message, prophetic words, healings and miracles.

Rudi & Carmen are closely knitted together with many other effective Christians, church fellowships, and groups of believers who share the same revelation and passion *to impart the truth of the gospel to others, and so* **to impact and transform the world we live in with the LOVE and POWER of God.**

www.ingramcontent.com/pod-product-compliance
Lightning Source LLC
Chambersburg PA
CBHW051837090426
42736CB00011B/1844